THE ENSERFMENT OF THE
RUSSIAN PEASANTRY

THE ENSERFMENT OF THE RUSSIAN PEASANTRY

R. E. F. SMITH

Professor of Russian
University of Birmingham

CAMBRIDGE
AT THE UNIVERSITY PRESS
1968

Published by the Syndics of the Cambridge University Press
Bentley House, P.O. Box 92, 200 Euston Road, London, N.W. 1
American Branch: 32 East 57th Street, New York, N.Y. 10022

© Cambridge University Press 1968

Standard Book Number: 521 07101 1

Printed in Great Britain
at the University Printing House, Cambridge
(Brooke Crutchley, University Printer)

CONTENTS

v

vi

vii

viii

ACKNOWLEDGEMENTS

I should like to thank those students and colleagues who have contributed so much to this book. I have been extremely fortunate in having the opportunity to discuss problems with colleagues in the Institute of History, Moscow. In particular I should like to thank S. M. Kashtanov, who took immense trouble to check my original draft and has answered numerous questions; his comments and suggestions have been invaluable to me. Any errors that remain are mine.

R. E. F. SMITH

ABBREVIATIONS

AAE	*Akty arkheograficheskoi ekspeditsii.*
AFZ i Kh	*Akty feodal'nogo zemlevladeniya i khozyaistva XIV–XVI vekov* (I–III, Izd-vo AN SSSR, M., 1951–61).
AI	*Akty istoricheskie.*
Akty Yushkova	*Akty XIII–XVII vv. predstavlennye v Razryadnyi prikaz* (ch. I, M., 1898).
ASEI	*Akty sotsial'no-ekonomichesko iistorii Severo-Vostochnoi Rusi* (I–III, Izd-vo AN SSSR, M., 1952–64).
D i DG	*Dukhovnye i dogovornye gramoty velikikh i udel'nykh knyazei XIV–XVI vv.* (Izd-vo AN SSSR, M.–L., 1950).
GVN i P	*Gramoty Velikogo Novgoroda i Pskova* (Izd-vo AN SSSR, M.–L., 1949).
IZ	*Istoricheskie zapiski.*
MIK XVI v	*Materialy po istorii krest'yan v russkom gosudarstve XVI veka* (Izd-vo LGU, 1955).
NG [year(s)]	*Novgorodskie gramoty na bereste (iz raskopok ... g.).* This is the general title; individual volumes which have been used in this work are:
	A. V. Artsikhovskii, B. I. Borkovskii, *(iz raskopok 1953–4 gg.)*, M., 1958.
	A. V. Artsikhovskii, B. I. Borkovskii, *(iz raskopok 1955 g.)*, M., 1958.
	A. V. Artsikhovskii, B. I. Borkovskii, *(iz raskopok 1956–7 gg.)*, M., 1963.
	A. V. Artsikhovskii, B. I. Borkovskii, *(iz raskopok 1958–61 gg.)*, M., 1963.
PI	*Problemy istochnikovedeniya.*

xii

PIK	*Pamyatniki istorii krest'yan XIV–XIX vv.* (*Pamyatniki russkoi istorii*, vi), M., 1910.
PRP	*Pamyatniki russkogo prava* (i–viii, Gosyurizdat, M., 1952–61.)
RIB	*Russkaya istoricheskaya biblioteka.*
SA	*Sovetskaya arkheologiya.*
ZhMNP	*Zhurnal Ministerstva narodnogo prosveshcheniya.*

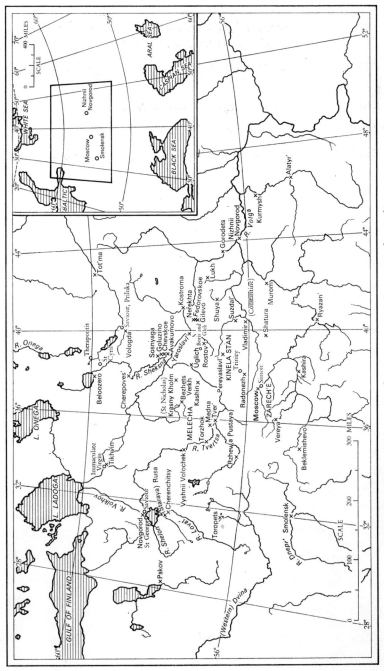

Central and northern area of European Russia.   Circles indicate monasteries

INTRODUCTION

A certain number of documents relevant to the study of social relations in what we now know as European Russia are available in west European languages. These include Professor G. Vernadsky's translation of Russian Law (*Russkaya Pravda*) and a number of other medieval legal enactments.[1] This gives us the opportunity to see some of the earliest evidence on the social structure of the East Slavs. The various Pravdas and their parts dated to different periods show us something of the changes which took place in social relations in the centuries preceding the Mongol invasions of the early thirteenth century. They also let us see something of the structure of administration on estates of princes and great noblemen, the boyars, and of the categories of dependants in the labour force on such estates. A number of early charters were translated into French by Alexander Eck,[2] and certain other documents including some ecclesiastical statutes are also available in French.[3] The Beloozero (White Lake) Charter, a local statute, is available in English in a translation by Dewey.[4]

The documents translated here have been selected in order to give the English reader some idea of the process by which peasants in the core of Russia came to be legally enserfed in the mid-seventeenth century. As far as possible the documents are presented in full. In this way the change from the frequently laconic and obscure nature of the earliest documents to the

[1] *Medieval Russian Laws*, no. XLI of the Records of Civilization, Sources and Studies (Columbia U.P., N.Y., 1947).

[2] *Le moyen âge russe* (Paris, 1933), pp. 475–93; this book also contains a useful index of Russian terms, pp. 564 f.

[3] M. Szeftel, *Documents de droit public relatifs à la Russie médiévale* (Bruxelles, 1963).

[4] H. W. Dewey, 'The White Lake Charter', *Speculum*, XXXII (1957), 79–83.

I

repetitive legalisms of the seventeenth century becomes quite clear. Moscow itself was originally a settlement of minor importance in the Rostov–Suzdal' area and the emergence of what is often referred to as a 'centralised state' in Russia was also the rise of Moscow to the headship of the Russian lands. The documents selected relate mainly to this central and northern area of European Russia (see the map on p. xiv) which the sixteenth-century English merchants knew as Muscovy. The reports of these merchants remain useful sources of information for some aspects of Russia at that time.[1] The western and southern areas lost to the Polish and Lithuanian states for most of the period under review are not dealt with here.

The glossary is intended to explain the main terms found in the texts and to enable those who wish to do so to learn what was the original Russian. About some terms, as Professor Vernadsky wrote, 'there still exists no consensus of opinion among scholars', but he was surely right when he rejected shifting the responsibility for translation from the translator to the reader. Russian history has too long been unfamiliar to readers of English; a sprinkling of Russian terms only helps to maintain the unfamiliarity and therefore an English expression has been used in preference to a Russian one, even when the former is used with a somewhat unusual meaning. The aim is to provide a translation of documents which will illustrate the process of enserfment in Russia. This little book is not intended as a critical text of the documents or an examination of the terminology, but the references given will, it is hoped, provide a starting-point for those who would like to pursue such matters.[2]

[1] See especially Richard Chancelor's account of Russia in Richard Hakluyt, *The Principal Navigations Voyages Traffiques & Discoveries of the English Nation*, (Glasgow, 1903), II, 224 f.; and Giles Fletcher, *Of the Russe Common Wealth in Russia at the close of the sixteenth century*, Hakluyt Society, 1st series, no. 20 (London, 1856). A recent facsimile edition with variants is: Giles Fletcher, *Of the Russe Commonwealth, 1591* (Cambridge, Mass., 1966).

[2] Some references to materials relating to terminology are given on pp. 164–5.

The historian who is more or less familiar with the history of serfdom in western Europe finds himself in a territory with few recognisable landmarks when he studies the documents of Russian serfdom. It should, however, be recognised that this unfamiliarity may to a considerable extent be due rather to the relative scantiness of the documentary evidence than to the strangeness of the phenomena which the documents describe or reflect. Peasant servility is a condition about which many sophisticated distinctions have been made, based, one sometimes feels, on variations of nomenclature rather than of reality. As a social phenomenon, however, its features are fairly straightforward and should not be difficult to recognise. Servile peasant families are to be distinguished from slaves, because the servile peasants have their own landed holdings from the produce of which they and their families live. True slaves possess no holdings and are fed and housed by their owners. Their labour is individual rather than family labour, and indeed the family itself is incompatible with full slavery. However, although the servile peasant family is economically self-sufficient, sharing this condition with the free peasant families, its servility is a product of a social system in which it is essential that part of the unfree peasants' time should be spent working for somebody else. It does not require much imagination to see that the payment of rent to a landlord, or taxes to the state, or the expenditure of labour on the lord's demesne, the king's highway or defence works, must be taken under the immediate or ultimate threat of force. Moreover, in so far as the relationships between social classes in stable societies are expressed in juridical terms, the enforced payment of rent or *corvée* from peasants who get nothing in return that they really need, will as likely as not be legitimated by the designation of the peasants as dependants, subordinates, that is serfs, of the superior power. Serfdom, therefore, is the legal expression of one of the means by which the ruling groups in a peasant society make sure that they get as big a share as they can of the product of peasant labour.

3

The documents which illustrate the history of the growth of Russian serfdom are largely concerned with the problems of limiting peasant movement and reclaiming peasant families who have fled. They are much less concerned with the actual mode of the exploitation of the peasants by the landowners, though such aspects of lord–peasant economic relationships as share-cropping and indebtedness do figure in these documents. On the other hand, the western European material on medieval serfdom is much more concerned with the exact form in which the product of peasant labour is turned into the income of the landlord. This does not mean of course, that the western lords and the western state powers did not concern themselves at all with the problem of peasant flight. Indeed, one of the interesting themes of twelfth and thirteenth century agrarian history in the West is the offering of relatively favourable terms of tenure, by lords who wanted to open up uncultivated land for colonisation, to peasants who might be dissatisfied with their too small holdings or too heavy rents and services. But the colonisation movement in the West should not be exaggerated. The amount of available land in no way compared with that in Russia. If England (to quote the late Mr R. V. Lennard) was in 1086 'an old country' so was the rest of western Europe. Compared with Russia it was (given the level of productive techniques) almost overpopulated. At this time the East Slav colonisation north of a line roughly from Ladoga to Murom was just getting under way. By the end of the thirteenth century in the West symptoms of peasant overpopulation recognisable in the con-temporary third world were widespread—dwarf holdings, shortage of meadow and pasture, shortage of livestock, shortage of manure.

The problems therefore for western landowners, at any rate before the demographic collapse of the mid-fourteenth century, was not to keep tenants, but how to get the most out of them. Correspondingly, the way in which the western peasants tried to defend themselves was not by flight but by organisation. By

4

this we do not mean simply the deliberate organisation of the occasional refusal of rents and services. Such refusal was the outcome of a social institution which, perhaps due to the small size and scattered nature of settlements, seems to have been comparatively weak in medieval Russia, however strongly it may have developed later. This was the village community. In the West it was not strong enough to prevent the enserfment of peasants by landowners, but was strong enough to limit severely the degree of exploitation, as the manorial custom of England, the *chartes-lois* of France and *Weisthümer* of western Germany demonstrate. These limitations, however, were imposed at the end of a very long and complex history of enserfment, going back through the dark ages and the imperial Roman era to prehistoric times when (as we assume from the archeological record) warrior aristocracies emerged to dominate tribal communities.

The beginnings of serfdom in western Europe are found in the dark ages, when the chaotic conditions of the times strengthened a domination by landowners of peasants who were already burdened by the legacy of ancient slavery. The authority of the state had little to do with this stage of enserfment.

The core of medieval serfdom was composed of the descendants of the slaves of Romanised western Europe. Even before the political collapse of the Empire these were being turned into servile peasants by being given holdings instead of being used as day-workers on the land which the landowners directly exploited. At the same time as economic advantage brought slavery nearer to serfdom, the descendants of the once free peasant farmers of the Romanised world, the *coloni*, were being deprived of freedom of movement and treated by the aristocracy and by the state as virtually servile. The upheavals of the barbarian invasions may have resulted in an increase in the number of those enslaved through war, but most of these were bound to be assimilated as peasant serfs rather than as real slaves, since the economies of the barbarian successor states to Rome could not have employed vast masses of slaves in their antique role. Some slaves were partially emancipated, other freemen were obliged to accept the domination of great land-owners, and a fairly homogeneous servile peasant class was formed. This general process is analogous to that in the Kiev state. Even so, western Europe under the hegemony of the Franks was not so dominated by the great noble and church estates as documentary survivals have led some historians to suppose. The *villa* organisation, it is true, with the close association of dependant peasant tenures and the large demesnes cultivated by tenants' labour services, was the main way in which the Frankish monarchy and aristocracy organised its economic resources. But evidence of land transfers during the feudalisation of European society between the tenth and twelfth centuries shows that there must have been many villages where the majority if not all of the peasant families were still legally free, even if economically much differentiated. For Russia we lack this sort of evidence, but the social situation of the peasant appears to have been similar.

The main form of serfdom in western Europe, then, up to about the tenth century was that which seemed to have as its main object the exaction of rents in labour, money and kind from peasant holdings organised within the framework of the big estates. The documentary evidence enumerates in great detail the pennies, the eggs, the hens, the loaves, the ale and so on that each peasant household had to provide for the lord; the number of days a week the men of the household had to work at ploughing, sowing, harrowing, reaping, mowing on the lord's demesne; and even the household goods that the women had to manufacture. But this system had to be considerably modified owing to a number of factors, such as the growth of production for the market, the devaluation of money rents, the fragmentation of peasant holdings, and the disintegration of the big estates. The modifications might have led to a reduction in the amount of peasant serfdom since demesne production was reduced in scale and tended to be done by hired rather than by servile labour (though to a lesser degree in England than on the continent). This, however, was not to be, for the feudal reorganisation of the period by no means reduced, but rather increased the power of the landlords as a class. This was in some ways a complex and contradictory process, because, whilst some of the feudal rulers were developing *their* power, the aristocrats, lay and ecclesiastical, were also increasing their private jurisdictions. This, in fact, was the means by which serfdom got a new lease of life, especially from the eleventh century. Again, we see a similar process from the fourteenth century in Russia, though modified by the defence needs of the state. If in the West peasants were no longer expected to hand over their surplus product as rent, roughly proportionate to their holding, they were now obliged to do so in the form of fines paid in the lord's private court, fees for the use of the lord's oven, mill, winepress, etc. (*banalités*), even labour services on the lord's land exacted by him now not from peasants as his tenants but from peasants as subjects to his jurisdiction. Indeed, a peasant could find himself paying these sums to an overlord whilst he paid a rent for his land to a different person.

This changed form of serfdom was characteristic particularly of Europe from the Rhineland westward. Conditions in Italy were peculiarly affected by the advanced degree of urbanisation; those in Spain by the Reconquest. The situation in England was again peculiar and deserves a little extra space. What has been said about Frankish Europe was probably generally true of pre-Conquest England, that is manorially organised estates supporting the Crown and the great nobles co-existing with a good deal of free peasant family property. On the big estates, as far as one can see, the tenants were geared to the cultivation of the demesne as in Francia. In addition, the Old English law codes suggest that there were still many household slaves who formed the core of the demesne labour. The conquest by the

Normans made little immediate difference, but in the first half of the twelfth century the same tendencies to the disintegration of the old estate organisation as on the continent began to be apparent. This did not go far, and the relationship between demesne and peasant tenures was maintained even if in practice landlords often preferred to take the money equivalent of the services owed. There was, however, an intensification of legal serfdom as on the continent, with an important difference in that on the continent this was done by the strengthening of the jurisdictional power of the lords. In England, although the lords did strengthen their jurisdictional powers at the manorial (or village) level the full extension of enserfment was achieved by the close co-operation of the landowners and the state, operating mainly through the justices in the common law courts.

The intensification of serfdom, with a special emphasis on the jurisdictional power of lords, took place between the eleventh and thirteenth centuries. The power of the state assisted the lords in England but was not particularly active (except that the kings were also landowners) on the continent. This was a period when, in spite of the colonisation movement, peasant flight was not a problem owing to the shortage of land. After the population collapse of the mid-fourteenth century, the situation completely changed. The relative abundance of holdings encouraged peasant mobility, so that there was a real problem for landowners who were short of both wage labour and tenants. How did they face the problem of peasant flight? In western Europe landowners neither by themselves nor with state aid were able to impose the eastern European solution of strengthened serfdom. They attempted to retain and attract tenants by reducing rents and by practically abolishing labour services. Two factors are prominent here. First, estate owners either leased out demesnes or used hired labour, often preferring to turn over to pastoral farming with its low labour costs. Hence forced labour services were not required. Second, the peasants themselves seem to have been able to exercise

8

enough resistance to make a forcible solution, that is the re-imposition of the stringent conditions of earlier serfdom, impossible. The nearest that the landowners and the state got, working in conjunction, was in the English wage legislation of 1349 and after, aimed at keeping the cost of hired labour down. This legislation also embodied restrictions on movement, but of wage labourers, not of tenants. By the sixteenth century, when the land/labour ratio began once again to militate against peasants of the traditional type, serfdom was still no solution. By now the development of the capitalist elements in the economy encouraged evictions, and instead of state-sponsored serfdom as in Russia, we have a continuation of the control of the wage labour force as expressed for instance in the labour legislation of Tudor governments.

When we turn to the Russian evidence, despite certain analogues, we are faced with many differences. The earliest section of Russian Law (*Russkaya Pravda*), generally regarded as dating from the first half of the eleventh century, shows us the blood feud with the alternative of a uniform money payment (forty grivnas) in cases of murder.[1] The term for 'man' (*muzh*) seems to have been analogous to the medieval law-Latin use of *homo* as a synonym of *baro;* thus the phrase 'If a man kills a man', with which *Russkaya Pravda* opens, relates only to lords in a broad sense. Later sections of this Law, dated to the late eleventh century, show a graduated series of money payments in murder cases. These are of interest as they tell us something of social structure. A similar series is found in sections of the law dated to the late twelfth century (see p. 10.)

At about A.D. 1000 East Slav colonisation was still proceeding, particularly in the north and north-east, and in the next two centuries vast territories in this area were brought within Novgorod's sphere of influence and gradually settled. At the

---

[1] For a commentary in English on *Russkaya Pravda* and the terminological problems involved see Professor G. Vernadsky's *Medieval Russian Laws* referred to on p. 1 n. 1.

Amount in grivnas	Late eleventh century	Late twelfth century
80	Steward, tax-collector, prince's servant, senior groom	Prince's man or servant, steward, groom
40		Merchant, boyar servant, administrator, a man without a commune, a person (*lyudin*), prince's retainer, groom or cook
12	Rural and arable overseers, slave tutor, nurse	Artisans, rural servant of prince, arable servant of prince, (slave) tutor or nurse
5	Contract man, dependent peasant, slave	Contract man, slave

same time as the bounds of Slav colonisation were being extended, internal colonisation and the extension of settlement were also taking place. Little is known about the means by which these processes occurred; there was princely encouragement in some cases, but much extension of settlement was probably due to natural increase in numbers of population and the pressure on resources which this involved. The custom of early marriage [see 46] was probably a major factor in this. There is also some slight evidence that as early as the tenth century some slaves were being put to work on the land.[1] Early in the eleventh century a new term appears in the sources, *kholop*, which is here translated as villein. This usage has been adopted from Fletcher, an English merchant in Russia in the sixteenth century, who translated the term as villein or bond slave; it should be remembered that in England villeins were not slaves in earlier centuries. The appearance of this category of slaves 'was connected with the growth of a feudally dependent peasantry' according to Cherepnin.[2] In the course of the eleventh and early twelfth centuries a number of measures

[1] Zimin, *Istoriya SSSR* (1965), VI, 53-4.   [2] *IZ*, LVI, 257.

tended to make the situation of villeins somewhat easier so that they came to approximate in social situation to dependent peasants; this was probably the reason for the term 'full villein' (*obelnyi kholop*) which is first found in the eleventh century in Vladimir Monomakh's section of the Expanded Pravda.[1] But while the general process of territorialisation which was taking place in these centuries may have led to some improvement in conditions for part of the former slave labour force (this seems to be suggested by a number of risings in the late eleventh and early twelfth centuries), we do not know anything of the numbers involved. Such improvement was probably more than counterbalanced by the extension of the lord's power over the free peasants.

Grekov regarded the term *smerd* as indicating the peasant with his own means of production, whatever his legal status.[2] Thus *smerd* could mean both the peasant in his commune 'subject only to the jurisdiction of the state', and the peasant who was dependent on a lord. Zimin, however, has pointed out that 'the free member of a commune is not once called *smerd* in Russian Law (members of a commune are most frequently referred to as "people", cp. article 19 of the Short Pravda, etc.). The Russian sources first begin to speak of *smerds* only in the early eleventh century and this is linked with the development of feudalisation (see the treaty of 1006 between Rus and the Bolgars where *smerdin* is mentioned, and also the entry in the Novgorod I Chronicle under 1016).'[3] Subsequently Cherepnin gave some consideration to the term 'people' (*lyudi*) as indicating 'the basic mass of the rural and urban population in the earliest sources' and Zimin has developed his criticism of Grekov's views on *smerd*.[4] According to Zimin 'the historical fate of the term "*smerd*" reminds us of the evolution of the term

---

[1] *PRP*, I, 167; Vernadsky, *Medieval Laws*, pp. 43 f.; the term occurs in article 63 and Vernadsky translates it as 'full slave'.

[2] Grekov, *Kiev Rus*, p. 286. Cp. Blum, *Lord and peasant*, p. 27.

[3] *PRP*, I, 99.

[4] Cherepnin, *IZ*, LVI, 236; Zimin, *Istoriko-arkheologicheskii sbornik*, pp. 222-7.

"*servus*": at first slave, subsequently serf. While in the eleventh century *smerds* were a category of princely villeins established on the land, gradually in the twelfth century they became servile peasants. The *smerds* succeeded in winning considerable concessions from the representatives of princely power in the course of the risings at the end of the eleventh and beginning of the twelfth centuries; thanks to this their situation approximated to that of the enserfed members of communes, but it continued not to coincide for a long time.'[1] In the Pskov area, however, *smerds* seem to have been 'peasant members of communes who were established on the lands of Lord Pskov' until the 1480s.[2] Then they became dependants of individual nobles, churches or monasteries. In Novgorod land the position of *smerds* seems to have been similar.[3] Cherepnin has suggested that this category of peasants who paid tribute to the state arose as a result of free land becoming state-owned.[4] It seems clear that in the Novgorod area at least the terms people (*lyudi*) and *smerds* were quite close in content, both indicating peasants who were at least liable to state taxation.

The evidence from Russian Law shows that by the late eleventh century there were some estates of princes and great nobles with overseers for the villages and for the arable land. Such estates, where they existed, had both contracted and slave labour, as well as dependent peasants on them; the latter are implied by the mention of rural and arable overseers. It is noteworthy that a 'man' in the sense of a 'person' (*lyudin*) is in the late twelfth century valued as highly as a merchant or a prince's official; this reflects the relatively high status of the free peasant. In later documents we shall frequently meet the plural of this term ('people', *lyudi*) in the sense of peasants and, later, of bond slaves. The Russian Law's concern with payments in murder cases was no doubt partly due to such payments being, relatively

[1] Zimin, *op. cit.* p. 227.
[2] Marasinova, *Novye Pskovskie gramoty XIV–XV vekov*, p. 162.
[3] Cherepnin, *IZ*, LVI, 246–7.   [4] *Ibid.* p. 248.

speaking, an innovation perhaps not yet accepted throughout society; but there was also the fact that justice provided income for those administering it [see document 1].

Little is known about the origin of great estates in Russia.[1] Little, too, is known of their internal organisation; what is known seems insufficient to support Blum's view of magnates engaging, possibly a good deal, in direct production for a market;[2] this may sometimes have taken place, but it was probably exceptional. The hierarchy of officials seen in the Expanded Pravda would be required even if there was little demesne and no production for the market. It seems altogether improbable that the great estates of these times were production units; they were a sort of management unit, extracting income from the peasants, including the large quantities of supplies required for household consumption. The basic production unit, however, was the peasant holding; the lord's holding may have been intermingled with those of the peasants.[3] Before the Mongol invasions of the thirteenth century such estates seem to have been worked by a labour force which included a variety of dependants of lowly status, slaves among them [2].

In the second half of the twelfth century a major shift took place in the life of the Kiev state. Kiev itself lost its former importance; the Dnepr river route from the north to Constantinople had declined, the route itself was exposed to attacks from the steppe nomads, the influx of coins from East and West ceased and the twelfth to fourteenth centuries are sometimes referred to as a moneyless period. The town was sacked in 1169 and the effective centre, in so far as there was one, shifted to Suzdal' in the north-east. The new area was to be part of that core of European Russia with which we are concerned in the documents presented here. By this time, too, the tribes seem to have been replaced by territorial units, though many cultural features long persisted. The former largely

---

[1] See Blum, *Speculum*, XXVIII, 781 f., and his *Lord and peasant in Russia*, p. 33.
[2] Blum, *Lord and peasant in Russia*, p. 43. [3] Smith, *Origins*, p. 171.

nominal unity of the Kiev state was replaced by a number of principalities. The shift in the focus of interest to the north-east reflects the growth of colonisation and town building by princes at least as much as it does the decline of the more southerly area. The decline of the twelfth to thirteenth centuries was not sufficient to halt the colonisation process.

The destruction and losses caused by the Mongol invasions of the early thirteenth century mainly affected the central areas of Vladimir and Suzdal' and the Kiev region; even in these areas the incidence of destruction varied. On present evidence it is unclear whether, or to what extent, there had been any overall economic decline before the Mongol invasions. Blum seems to imply that an economic decline and a fall in population took place from the thirteenth to the fifteenth centuries, presumably after the Mongol attacks.[1] His most plentiful evidence for this decline is the large number of references in fourteenth and fifteenth century documents to *pustoshi*, a term which he takes to mean abandoned lands. In fact, however, the term can mean either abandoned lands or lands which have no one dwelling on them (*pustoi* being contrasted with *zhivushchii*). The evidence on wastes, therefore, might sometimes be an indication of intensive colonisation, the first step in establishing a new tenement being the use or cultivation of some patch in the forest at which there was as yet no house. Moreover, in these centuries there is much positive evidence for new land being brought into cultivation. Furthermore, it was in the second half of the fourteenth century that minting of coins started in several principalities. In the fifteenth century there is more evidence of peasants renting land to work. Such indications suggest boom rather than slump.

Our sources, while implying a labour force on estates after the Mongol invasions, do not always record it [3]; this again

[1] *Lord and peasant in Russia*, pp. 60–1. A useful survey of the evidence on the long-term imposition of taxation by the Mongols is given by M. Roublev, *Cahiers du monde russe et soviétique*, VII, 487–530.

does not suggest a severe labour shortage. Princes and great nobles continued to have slaves [5]; but there appears to be no evidence for men enserfed as a result of debts. The word generally used to indicate peasants seems to have been 'people' [4, 9]; 'orphans' was another term which had a similar meaning [7]. The surviving documents of this period, which probably do not adequately illustrate the century and a half immediately following the invasions, show us a continuing series of attempts to define the relationships between peasants and their lords whether the former paid rent in kind [6], or owed labour services, or both [9, 21]. Increasingly, in the early fifteenth century, attempts were made by the major landlords, such as the princes, both lay and clerical, to compile registers of peasants on their own estates [10, 13, 20, 24, 28]; the bounds of the latter were also sometimes more narrowly defined than seems to have been customary hitherto [11]. This change seems most probably to have been due to an increase in density of settlement, but the spread of more intensive techniques may sometimes have contributed to it.

Evidence on settlement size is fairly clear, even though it is still inadequate in many ways. Settlements were generally smaller in Russia than in England.[1] There may even have been a decline in settlement size in some areas after the Mongol invasions; there also seems to have been a temporary halt to the growth of the number of towns. There may, therefore, have been an increase in the number of very small settlements accompanying this hiatus in town building or there may have been a decline in population. It seems clear, however, that some colonisation was taking place throughout the whole period with which we are dealing, though it remains impossible to indicate its scale at different times.

We have, then, little evidence for any overall decline in European Russia in the twelfth to fifteenth centuries, even though this was a period of major changes. The tribal structure

---

[1] *Cambridge Economic History of Europe* (2nd ed.), I, 514–17, 521.

of society had already given way to one of principalities, territorialisation had proceeded far and may have been stimulated by the decline in the importance of the Dnepr river route to Constantinople and also by the halt to the growth of towns in the thirteenth century. Throughout this period, however, the multiplication of peasant tenements seems to have contributed to colonisation and settlement of an increasing area of the East European plain; it was these tenements which were the basic production units. The evidence we have, however, needs supplementing considerably before anything like a complete picture can be drawn even in outline.

In the early stages of this general process, peasants still evidently felt they had the right to a say in the disposition of the land off which they lived [8]. In the early fifteenth century peasants, moreover, were evidently still able to move from one lord to another [12]. There is also some evidence for peasants holding heritable estates and being able to write [15].[1] The land continued to be regarded as family rather than individual property [19, 29]; it was as if those who worked the land or exploited those who did so, who lived on it and made their livelihood from it, thereby had rights in the land, irrespective of any claims to ownership or power made by overlords. The tradition of the comparatively high status of the free peasant still continued to have some influence. The family was the basic unit of society; the tribe had been long outlived as an effective social unit [3]. But the family was of importance not only as a social unit; it was also the basic economic production unit. It could determine to whom a man was subject in certain circumstances; it was the unit which provided a man's bread [10], and was the normal individual work unit on estates throughout the period dealt with here [46, 49, 56]. The phrase 'to live' itself implied making a living by working the land, directly

[1] It has recently been suggested that a category of peasants holding land by inheritance, *dedichi*, were known in the Smolensk region in the twelfth century. See D. and A. Poppe, *Kwartalnik historyczny*, LXXIV, 1, 3–19.

16

in the case of peasants [20], indirectly in the case of lords [24].[1]

There is evidence, from the first half of the fifteenth century, of peasants fleeing from an estate as a result of excessive impositions [16]. It may be significant that this evidence is from the economically more advanced Novgorod area. At the same period in the Pereyaslavl' region 'people', i.e. peasants, were attracted to estates by being granted exemption from certain obligations, usually for a limited period [14, 18, 20]. Such measures suggest that landlords, at least in certain areas, were experiencing a labour shortage which in some circumstances led them to increase their demands on their peasants and in others forced them to offer advantageous terms in order to attract newcomers. Both aspects may be associated with this period of development following the recuperation from the Mongol invasions. The principality of Moscow had started to acquire additional territory in the early fourteenth century. At the death of Vasilii II the gathering of the principalities of central and north European Russia under Moscow's dominion now included all but Novgorod, Tver', Rostov and Ryazan'. By 1480, the year traditionally regarded as the final overthrow of Mongol domination, Perm' and the wealthy Novgorod had been included in Moscow's rule. Tver' was added in 1485 and Vyatka in 1489. Thus the second half of the fifteenth century was a crucial period in the growth of Moscow's political authority and power. This process is to be linked with the increasing pressure of lord on peasant. As the state developed and military and other demands increased so did the pressure of the lord on his peasants.

The greater the number of peasant tenements on an estate, the greater the income was likely to be; hence, the continual impetus to seek and retain peasants felt by all types of landlord. Peasants on such estates now fell into two broad categories: old-established peasants, who were already living on the estate

[1] Cherepnin, *IZ*, LVI, 244; also his *Obrazovanie*, pp. 212–16.

and, perhaps, registered there; and arrivals, those who had been 'called' from other parts, attracted by easier conditions including the establishment of free settlements where relaxations of taxation and other obligations operated [17]. This categorisation, however, seems to have been a workaday one and not at all narrowly juridical at this period. The two categories as it were reflect the two conflicting aspects of the policy of landlords having to provide conditions hard enough to give them what they considered an adequate income, but easy enough to attract settlers.

Shortly after the middle of the fifteenth century control of peasant movement began to be more pronounced. By 1460 the Grand Prince's 'registered and unregistered people' were not to be accepted by other lords [10]. At about the same time the Trinity Monastery of St Sergius, the largest monastery in Russia was authorised not to allow its peasants to withdraw from one of its estates to those of other lords [22]. Another charter at this time authorised the return of peasants who had left the Monastery's estate in order to avoid defence duties [23]. A will of a Grand Prince ordered inquisitions to be carried out into the lands inherited by his heirs so as to tax 'by sokha-units and people' [24]. This is an instruction close to those which authorised the detailed and extensive inquisitions which were carried out in most parts of European Russia during the following two centuries [38]. An instruction of this type from the middle of the seventeenth century is included later [54].

A particular aspect of this increasing control around 1460 was the restriction of the movement of share-croppers, and of a new category, those paying rents or loan repayments in money ('silver-men'), and those on contract. In one document at this period silver-men were to have the right to move only during three weeks about the autumn St George's day (26 November)[1] [25]. Another similarly restricted to St George's day the movement of both share-croppers, money-paying people and those

---

[1] Old Style, as for all dates given in the documents.

on contract [26]. Almost at the same time the movement of peasants ('people') in general on one of the Trinity Monastery estates was limited to two weeks in the early winter [27; cp. 30, 31]. Moreover, another grant in the 1460s excluded 'any tribute paying people who are registered' from those allowed exemption from obligations [28]. Thus, around 1460, registration had begun to be used to limit the peasant right to move in order to acquire such temporary benefits. It is at about this time, too, that the term 'fully enslaved people' came into use [29]. The unqualified term *kholop*, which Fletcher, an English merchant in Russia in the sixteenth century translated as villein or bond slave, had lost some of its former significance. By the late fifteenth century some who were nominally such approximated in status to some dependent peasants, even though the latter were subject to tax (*tyaglie*) and the former were not. The right to move, however, was severely restricted, if not entirely absent, for both. Social changes, including the increasing use of money, itself evidence of the fifteenth-century economic advance, led to many indenturing themselves as peasants on contract or as fully enslaved people [29, 33, 34]. Some categories of these had agricultural holdings, though others were in-servants or field workers without land. All were regarded as servile, though at different times and under different contracts the period of servitude differed. These dependants (*kholopy*) are here called villeins, since Fletcher's use of the term seems adequately to reflect the servile status of most of them.

It seems probable that by the late 1480s the restriction of peasant movement to a period around the autumn St George's day was sufficiently well-established for it not necessarily to be mentioned expressly where one would expect to find it [32]. By this time it is quite clear that the withdrawal of money-paying peasants from one estate to another and the indenturing of villeins was, in fact, often a financial transaction between the lords; the sale of himself by peasant or villein was merely a legal fiction [33, 34]. Normally, the only way out of the debt which reduced a man to servile status was for another lord to pay it; the man himself was unable to accumulate the sum required.

The Law Code of 1497 summed up the changes we have so far seen reflected in charters and deeds relating to individual estates; it laid down regulations applying to the whole of the rapidly growing area under the rule of Moscow [35]. In particular, it laid down that peasants could move only in the week before and the week after the autumn St George's day; before they could leave they also had to pay an amount, graduated for the first four years of residence and differing according to whether the tenement was on open land or in the forest. This first legal code of the state as a whole both unified the developments which had taken place in the second half of the fifteenth century and, by strengthening the central authority, laid the basis for further changes.

The increasing power of central authority gradually and in piecemeal fashion asserted itself over the rights of those holding immunities [36]. Enserfment for debt took place and the deeds recording such contracts in the early sixteenth century included provisions aimed at restricting the means of escape [37,41]. One such means was to obtain a terminable privilege [39]. By the middle of the sixteenth century, however, no fundamental change in social organisation, as reflected in legal documents, had occurred. In this sense the extract from an inquisition describing an estate held by service on which there were villein and peasant dependants may be regarded as fairly typical [38]. When a new Law Code was issued in 1550 the provision on peasant movement remained fundamentally the same, though an attempt was made to introduce more precision into the regulations [40]. Villeins, however, were now allowed to move without term; this suggests that lords still frequently had such dependants on their manors and the government at this point felt it necessary to make a concession to them.

In the course of the sixteenth century, however, and particularly in the second half, the system of estates held by service became much more developed. The crown based itself on this system of making land grants to servitors in return for their service, which was usually, but not always, military.

Land allowance to servitors

(Chets per field)

	Moscow area				Other towns
	1 1550	2 1587	3 1626	4 1649	5 Seventeenth century
Boyars	200	200	—	200	1000
Chamberlains	200	—	—	150	900–750
Clerks to the Council	—	—	—	150	—
Patriarch's Chamberlains	—	—	100	—	—
Sewers	200	100	—	100	—
Bearers of insignia	—	100	—	100	1500–600
Moscow gentlemen	—	100	—	100	900–700
Clerks	—	—	—	100	—
Moscow musketeer commanders	—	60	—	100	250–100
Gentlemen selected from the towns	—	50	—	70	700–300★
Junior boyars	200, 150 or 100	—	—	—	—
Junior clerks	—	50	—	—	—
Attendants, stirrup grooms, Moscow musketeer officers	—	—	—	50	250–100†
Court people, stirrup men, officers of the tsar's drinks, junior boyar officers of the tsarina	—	—	—	100–10	—

★ Scales of grants of overgrown or virgin land in border areas (supplementary grants in brackets) were: 400 (70), 300 (60), 250 (50), 200 (40), 150 (40), 100 (30), 70 (25).
† Moscow musketeer officers.

Sources:
1   A. A. Zimin, *Tysyachnaya kniga 1550g.*, pp. 53–5.
2   *PRP*, v, 434–5.
3   *PRP*, v, 486.
4   *Sobornoe Ulozhenie 1649g.*, xvi, § 1, in *PRP*, vi, 202.
5   *PRP*, v, 486; *Sobornoe Ulozhenie 1649g.*, xvi, § 40, in *PRP*, vi, 210–11.

In 1550 and again in 1587 standard allotments of land were laid down varying according to the rank of the recipient; they applied to servitors with estates in an area about 40–50 miles around Moscow. Such a system, first established when Ivan IV granted lands to the 'chosen thousand' of his special force (*oprichnina*), was further developed with modifications in the seventeenth century. By that time grants of between 40 and 100 chets in each of the three fields, perhaps 5–17 peasant tenements, were considered small (see the Law Code of 1649, Chap. XVI, §22). The figures given in the table (p. 21) were often exceeded in reality, in part because the quality of land was taken into account. Land was classed as 'good', 'average' or 'poor'. If supplementary grants could be made, recipients with average lands might have 125, for every 100 units allotted, while those with poor lands might have 150 (*ibid.*, §48).

The development of the local administration from the early sixteenth century, when immunities and livings were being brought under closer control [36], was accompanied by the emergence of a central administration which in the second half of the century became increasingly functional rather than territorial. This growth of the administration, together with the emergence of the standard system of service estates, with close control by a government department to ensure that service was performed, led to new pressure by the servitors on the peasants living on these estates.

Monasteries lent considerable sums and expected to receive large amounts of both money and grain in return; but the destruction of the agricultural resources of the central areas and the flight of increasing numbers of peasants, both of which had been caused by the havoc resulting from the *oprichnina* of Ivan IV, were already being felt in the 1580s [43]. While all prices rose at the end of the 1570s, the price of grain in particular leapt up in the 1580s. Towards the end of the sixteenth century, however, partly as a result of the flight of increasing numbers of peasants and the consequent shift in the land/labour ratio, new elements in the situation appear. At the same time there were conflicts of interest between the old, boyar families sometimes with large estates and many resources, and the more numerous new, smaller servitors with fewer resources, who were frequently involved in campaigns and therefore absent from their estates, sometimes for years at a time [see 39, 51, 54].

The lords' continuing search for additions to their labour force at times led to the use of violence and other abuses [42]. This conflict between the servitors themselves, and the servitors' continual demand for an extension of their right to villeins and peasants, is ever present in the late sixteenth and first half of the seventeenth centuries.

From this time the language of the documents changes [cp. for example, 42, 44]. The royal bureaucracy, though still fairly simple in structure, had already elaborated a new juridical language and this reflects a changed social situation. Much more important, however, than the appearance of this restricted language code, are the changes in content. Possibly from as far back as 1581, when the labour shortage was already being felt, there had been various temporary remissions of the peasant right of departure; after a number of such forbidden years a decree was passed in 1597, as a result of pressure from the servitors, giving landlords the right to search for and reclaim any peasants who had run away. They were given five years in which to do so [44]. In 1592 and 1593 a number of extensive inquisitions had been held; the registers of these would serve as a basis for reference in any disputes.

The start of the seventeenth century in Russian history is known loosely as the Time of Troubles. There were famines in the central areas in 1601–3; these, as well as social pressures, contributed to a peasant rising led by a certain Khlopka in 1603. The following year the Poles invaded, partly induced by the prospect of income from estates supplying grain to the Baltic trade, and captured Moscow, which they held until 1612. There was a fairly widespread peasant rising led by Bolotnikov in 1606–7. During the Time of Troubles, the Tsar felt obliged to make concessions both to the peasants, who were again granted the right to move, and to the servitors, who were also allowed to move one or two peasants [see 45]. This decree, subsequently claimed to be illegal because it had been issued without the boyar assent, was in any event confusing. It was rescinded in

1607 when a fifteen-year right of search was granted, again on the basis of the inquisitions of 1592 and 1593 [46].

The peasant situation in general had deteriorated as the authority of the state and of those holding estates by service grew. The distinctions between peasants and villeins were becoming blurred. Peasants came to be sold or 'conceded' from one estate to another [47]; they were thus in effect being sold without land. Their lords controlled their marriages and even disposed of their unborn children [48]. Thus, on estates and in the violent conflicts between the various categories of landlords [49], the peasant had come to be treated almost like a slave, even though he was still not legally enserfed. Peasants still contracted loans and this was one way in which their own status [53] or that of their children [55] might decline to that of a bond slave.

By the seventeenth century the documents offer us an established and complex terminology for the various social categories [see 45, 50]. Servitors might be divided into the men of the council (boyars, chamberlains and others), and other servitors. The latter, the gentlemen, were subdivided into those attendant in the capital (the Moscow ranks) and those of other towns, the town, of course, representing an area. Next in the social scale were those subject to taxation, that is the commons, the rank and file of town and countryside (cp. the earlier meaning of 'people' (*lyudi*)), including the peasants. Lower still were those not liable to state taxes, the villeins, and also the vagabonds and others not incorporated in their own right into the social hierarchy. Villeinage seems to have been on the increase in the first half of the seventeenth century; at least there is evidence of some forms of servile dependence not previously known. Notes for livelihood (when the lord supplied livery and diet in return for service) or for loans, as well as bondage deeds, were some of the means by which a relationship of servitude could be established. Even hiring oneself out for work evidently in reality might lead to such dependence; the law had expressly to forbid villeinage resulting from hire [56, §32].

24

From the second quarter of the seventeenth century onwards, once the immediate impact of the Time of Troubles was over, the final phases of the enserfment began. Various periods were decreed at different times within which runaway peasants might be legally reclaimed [50, 51]. By this time, it should be noted, 'peasant' has come virtually to mean serf, in the sense that the right of departure is no longer fundamentally recognised. The term 'people' now is either used in a broad sense as often in the documents given here, or continues, as in the inquisitions, to signify villeins as it had in [38].

It seems profitless to go into the details of the various periods decreed for the right of search at this time. Even at the start of the 1640s, however, limited periods were still being decreed, despite the appeal of the smaller-scale land holders for the right of search without term [52]. It is true that in 1646 a document was issued granting the right of search without term, but this seems to have applied only to the Moscow uezd [54]. This document is of interest in that it gives us a clear picture of the measures taken when organising inquisitions, and tells us something of the counter-measures undertaken by landlords.

In 1648 there were disturbances and riots in Moscow and in several other parts of European Russia, as well as in Siberia. While these were mainly centred on the artisan quarters of the towns, and were utilised by the gentlemen assembled for a military campaign to urge their interests, in a few cases peasants joined in as well. There had been similar disturbances and submissions of collective petitions in some earlier years, but this was the first time that the Moscow gentlemen and the attendants had participated. The result, in part, of these disturbances, in part of the conflict between the various categories of landlords for work hands, was the calling of an Assembly of the Land which met in 1649 and finally completed the enserfment of the peasantry [56]. This was done by allowing the right of search without term. Thus, the Russian peasant was finally bound not to the land, but to his master.

In Russia, then, the peasant underwent a process of increasing control between the tenth and the seventeenth centuries ending with legal enserfment. The contrast with west European experience is marked; the Code of Laws finally enserfing the Russian peasant and the execution of Charles I both took place within a few weeks of one another in 1649. At first free peasants had high status, though in the tenth to twelfth centuries estates with servile labour, both slave and serf, also existed. The decline of Kiev, and the 'moneyless period' of the twelfth to fourteenth centuries, however, do not appear to have hindered the colonising movement. Moreover, other areas, such as the central areas and Novgorod which was associated with the Baltic trade, continued to develop. In fact, the halt in the development of town life, or rather the *continuation* of the peasant tenement as the basic social and economic unit, probably mitigated the impact of such disasters as the Mongol invasions and the warfare between princes, though these led to increased concern for defence rather than other aspects of development. There seems little evidence of any deep and far-reaching crisis similar to that in western Europe in the fourteenth century despite the Mongol invasions. The population collapse in the West had no close parallel in the East, probably due at least in part to the different marriage pattern. Instead the fourteenth and fifteenth centuries were a period when Moscow became powerful enough to challenge and overthrow the Mongol overlordship. This was accompanied by increasing control of certain categories of peasants on the larger estates.

The end of Novgorod as an independent power in the late fifteenth century considerably strengthened Moscow. Novgorod's positive balance of trade with the West had resulted in considerable accumulations of precious metal, a situation to be found in other Russian trading towns. The acquisition of this additional wealth, as well as of Novgorod's vast territories coincided with the development of the system of tenure by service. This influx of precious metal occurred together with the growth of the internal market, of features which Makovskii has recently argued should be regarded as embryonic capitalism and of the importance of foreign trade. All this contributed to an increase in impositions and restrictions on the peasants in the sixteenth century. It should be noted, incidentally, that the development in the sixteenth century of regular trade in a wide range of goods with Iran, Turkey, the Nogai Horde and the Uzbek khanates was particularly important. While Russia has sometimes been regarded as a semi-colonial supplier of raw materials to the West at this time, to the Orient Russia was a supplier of manufactured goods as well as of raw materials. In this trade, too, Russia probably had a favourable balance. By this time Moscow's authority enabled laws to be issued relating to the whole state, which further controlled peasant movement and peasant–lord relations. All these developments were reflected in the price increases of the sixteenth century, which were more marked in the case of agricultural produce than for either artisan production or the produce of extractive activities. The demand for agricultural produce was evidently great enough to ensure quite a rapid recovery from the disasters of the late sixteenth and early seventeenth centuries. It was this demand, stimulated by the growth of the town, especially the artisan population, as well as by the increased pressure from an expanding state, soon to become an Empire, that provided the background to the final stages of the enserfment. Thus, in Russia we see in these centuries a somewhat similar development to that which had already taken place in the Baltic countries. But while in the Baltic area the phenomena labelled the second serfdom may have been mediated by trade, for most of European Russia trade, though perhaps more important than was formerly thought, seems to have played a smaller part than the military needs of the state.

R. H. HILTON
R. E. F. SMITH

I

This is the earliest original deed which has survived in Russia. The sources of income from the village which the Grand Prince and his son give to the monastery are the tribute normally paid to the overlord—namely, income from justice (bloodwites, that is compensation paid for murder, and fines, the latter probably being a recent innovation) and various other imposts, such as the marriage tax payable by the bride's parents and the autumn tributary gift, probably given when the lord or his officials made a progress round the estate. Dependence is here indicated only in a general liability to various impositions.

1125–32. Deed of the Grand Prince Mstislav Vladimirovich and his son Vsevolod giving the village of Buitse, tribute and a silver dish to the St George Monastery, Novgorod

GVN i P, no. 81

Now I, Mstislav, son of Vladimir, ruling the land of Rus'[1] in my reign have ordered my son Vsevolod to hand over Buitse to St George with tribute, bloodwites, fines and the . . .[2] marriage tax. And should any prince after my reign wish to take it back from St George, may God prevent that, and the Holy Virgin and that St George from whom he takes it back. And you, Abbot Isai, and you, brethren, while this world shall stand

[1] The term Russia (*Rossiya*) does not come into use till the sixteenth century. The precise significance of the earlier term Rus' is a matter of considerable dispute; it appears to have had ethnic, rather than administrative overtones.
[2] The gap was formerly read by different scholars as Vot, a Finnish tribe, or Volok, a place-name meaning the Portage. In any event, the words after 'fines' are a later insertion.

pray to God for me and my children, whoever shall remain in the monastery, you should pray God for us in life and in death. And I have also given with my hand the autumn tributary gift, twenty-five grivnas[1] to St George. And now I, Vsevolod, have given a silver dish of 30 grivnas of silver[2] to St George; I have ordered it to be struck at dinner, when the abbot dines.[3] And if anyone violates either that tribute or this dish, let God ïudge him on the day of his coming and also St George.

2

This is the earliest private document which has survived. It is probably typical of gifts to monasteries from the well-to-do who held estates and had dependants; these gifts were usually made either on being shorn as a monk or on death. Varlaam became a monk in 1192 and died in 1211; hence the two possible dates of the document.

The term 'household' (*chelyad'*) indicated the servile dependants, whether domestics or field workers. The fact that they are here associated with livestock suggests their lowly status and this seems to be borne out by the list of persons and stock given. For a convenient survey of servile dependants in early Russia see A. A. Zimin's article in *Istoriya SSSR* (1965), no. 6, pp. 39–75.

[1] = 6¼ silver grivnas. In 1229 the life of a free man was valued at 10 silver grivnas in a treaty between a prince of Smolensk and the Germans. See V. L. Yanin, *Denezhno-vesovye sistemy russkogo srednevekov'ya* (1956), p. 43. In a late twelfth-century treaty between Novgorod and Gotland the payment for the murder of an ambassador was 20 silver grivnas. See *GVN i P*, no. 28, p. 55. The silver grivna was the equivalent of four ordinary grivnas.

[2] Taking the silver grivna to be equal at this date to 204·756 grammes, the dish weighed about 6 kg. See Yanin, *op. cit.* p. 46.

[3] It was apparently customary for a dish to be struck or a bell sounded when food was brought into the refectory.

Possibly 1192 or 1211. Deed of gift of Varlaam to the Saviour Monastery, Khutynsk, of land, appurtenances, household and livestock

GVN i P, no. 104

Now Varlaam has given to the Holy Saviour land and a vegetable garden, fisheries and duck[1] runs and meadows: (1) the water meadow opposite the village over the Volkhov; (2) on the Volkhov weir; (3) root; (4) willow; (5) the small willow; (6) on the island and with the cornfields.[2]

He gave that Khutinsk land to the Holy Saviour with the household and livestock. And he gave to the brethren: (1) a retainer and his wife; (2) Voles; (3) the girl Fevroniya and two sons; (4) Nedach' and six horses and a cow. This is another village on the Sluditsa...gave to the Holy Saviour, and the church of St George in it, the cornfields and meadows and fisheries and weirs in it. All this Varlaam son of Mikhail gave to the Holy Saviour. If anyone instigated by the Devil and evil men wishes to deprive them of anything, the cornfields or the water-meadows or the fisheries, let the Holy Saviour be hostile both in this and in future ages.

3

Frequently early documents make no specific reference to the inhabitants of villages who worked the fields or to domestics. Yet the income from an estate, such as the one in this will, part of which was to support the widow, derived in all probability from a variety of obligations on the estate population. Moreover, the sums loaned out would produce quite considerable amounts of income, but there is no indication here of anything like enserfment on account of debt.

---

[1] The term *gogol'* indicates the Goldeneye (*Anas clangula*).
[2] Items (3), (4) and (5) in this list might possibly be place-names.

Not later than 1270. Testament of Kliment

GVN i P, no. 105

In the name of the Father, the Son and the Holy Ghost. Now I, Kliment, slave of God, [give] to St George and the abbot Varlam and all the brethren, since I took on loan 20 silver grivnas[1] from St George, there should be something with which to pay. I give for all that two villages with their stocks,[2] and with horses and with bee-trees, and with the small sites,[3] both stump and log, in full possession to St George; and the boundary man is my neighbour Opal'. And to Kalist I have given the village of Mikshino with its vegetable garden and bee-trees. And to Andrei, son of Voin, I give Samuilov village, both stump and... bee-trees. And I have given [this] not for nothing [since] Danilo and Voin paid the Lithuanian ransom for me. To Volodislav Danilovich I give the dark grey stallion and to brother Vasilii I give Voin's shield, also Venyamin's foal. And I order my wife to abbot Varlam and all the brethren. And from my pigs give Samuel the best boar; and the livestock, the sheep and the pigs are to be divided in half with my wife. And if my wife is to be shorn as a nun, she has something with which to be shorn and I also give her the town tenement. And about this I beg the abbot and all the brethren; if my wife is shorn as a nun, give her a quarter so that she shall not be hungry; if she does not obey this, give her something less. If I have anything remaining, a hinney or weapon, I give everything to St George. As for the money with which I had to pay you: take 8 grivnas from Foma in the merchant guild and 4 grivnas from Borka, 2 grivnas less 2 nogatas[4] from Foma Moroshnya

[1] One silver grivna equalled four grivnas of kunas; the latter were usually referred to simply as 'grivnas'.
[2] *Lit.* 'abundance' (*obilie*), i.e. corn.
[3] Presumably former hamlets or clearances administratively subordinate to the two villages.   [4] 1 grivna = 20 nogatas = 50 kunas or rezanas.

separately and Kliment is to take from Borka 13 nogatas and a grivna interest on the silver tribute and Kliment and Borka are to take five grivnas from Savinitse, and in that Borka a third, and Kliment is to take from Koza Votish 2 grivnas, and 40 rezanas from Mikiforich, and Zhikhnev…Kliment is to take from Khot'vit a grivna of salt money, half a grivna from Koch'n, and K…and half a grivna, half a grivna from Kozelich Lamlyana, 7 grivnas on Duran, half a grivna from Mikhalits, 2 grivnas less 10 rezanas from Eremei, 13 nogatas from Gyurya, and a grivna from Kliment, a grivna from Votish. If anyone shall attempt to go against this, let him stand with me before God. And you, Varlam, carry it out; I have written it since I have neither brother, nor son. If anyone violates this deed let him stand before God not with me alone, but with all my tribe.[1]

4

The letters, inscribed on thick birch bark with a stylus, which have been found in excavations at Novgorod and some other Russian sites are a remarkable source. They frequently throw light on phenomena at a lower social level than that reflected in the chronicles, the laws and other legal documents.

This is one such from Novgorod. The details are obscure, but it evidently refers to a disagreement between landowners engaged in a loan transaction. The rye which Mark is to take may possibly have been the interest on the loan. Both parties have control of 'people', a term frequently meaning 'peasants', but we do not know with any certainty the status of anyone mentioned in the document. The tree-ring date of the timber roadway at the level at which this letter was found is 1299 or 1306. On the tree-ring dating evidence see B. A. Kolchin, 'Dendrokhronologiya Novgoroda', *SA* (1962), 1, 113–39.

[1] By this period the East Slav tribes had long disappeared, but the family remained the basic unit of the economy as well as of society throughout the period dealt with here [see 10, 46, 56]. The kin group also had some continuing importance as regards the disposal of landed [19, 29] and other property [47].

Late thirteenth century. Novgorod birch bark letter no. 142

NG (1955)

Fom Joseph to Onfim. If Oleksa will send you from Mark the people, or to my wife, answer him thus: as you have agreed with me, Mark, I will ride out on St Peter's day[1] to you and look over my village and you are to take your rye and I will give you the interest, the capital has been given. And if I send the plough shares, you give them my blue horses, give them with the people without harnessing them to the *sokhi*.[2] And if he does not take them, let them into the herd in front of the people. Let the case rest with him, not me. And I myself will consult with him.

5

This is a treaty between the town of Novgorod and its prince. About thirty such are known, but none go back to the period after the rising of 1136 when such arrangements began to be elaborated. The earliest surviving treaty is not earlier than 1 March 1264. (On the dates of these treaties see A. A. Zimin, *PI*, v, 300–27.) The town was largely dominated by the great nobles (boyars) and the merchants who were able to limit the power of the prince. Any villages which the prince holds in his own right, or through his family or court, are to be given up. The word of a villein or slave of either sex is not to be accepted if it is against the master. Neither villeins nor share-croppers (literally 'halvers', i.e. those paying half or some other fixed proportion of their harvest as rent) are able to stand in court independently of their master; they apparently do not exist as legal entities in this respect.

---

[1] 29 June. St Peter's day was the customary summer quarter day as Christmas was the winter one. See no. 10, §11.

[2] *Sokha*, pl. *sokhi*, is a wooden implement, an ard with two or more prongs or, as here, share-beams. It remained a standard implement of the Russian peasant until the 1920s.

Between 27 July 1304 and 28 February 1305. Document with treaty conditions
[GVN i P, no. 7

Blessings from the Archbishop, greetings from the town head Georgii and from the thousand man[1] Andreïya and from all elders and from all juniors and from all Novgorod to the lord Prince Mikhail Yaroslavich. You are to kiss the cross to this, prince, to all Novgorod, to what the first princes kissed the cross and your grandfather and your father. You are to rule Novgorod in accordance with custom, as your grandfather and your father ruled it. You are not to annul documents. And you are not to deprive a man of his volost[2] without fault. And you are not to distribute volosts without the town head, nor to administer justice, nor to grant deeds. And you, prince, are not to rule the Novgorod volosts with your men, you are to rule them with Novgorod men; and you are to have a gift from those volosts: And these are the Novgorod volosts: Volok [= the Portage] with all its volosts, and you are to hold your servant on half and a Novgorod man on half in all the Volok volost; and in Torzhok, prince, you are to hold your servant on your part and a Novgorod man on his part. And these are the Novgorod volosts; Bezhets, Gorodets', Melecha, Shipino, Egna, Vologda, Zavolochie, Koloperm', T're, Perm', Pechera, Yugra; and you are to rule these volosts with Novgorod men. And, prince, you are to hunt pigs 60 verstas[3] round the town and further where it suits anyone. And you are not to accept persons commending themselves, prince, anywhere in the Nov-

---

[1] The thousand-man (*tysyatskii*) was responsible for the armed forces and the trade court in Novgorod.

[2] A volost (*volost'*) was an administrative division, sometimes within a larger unit called an uezd. In a looser sense, however, it signified any area under a single individual. Thus it could sometimes refer to a single estate [see 10], p. 42 n. 1.

[3] A versta was approximately two-thirds of a mile, so the restriction applied to roughly forty miles.

34

gorod volosts, nor is your princess, nor are your boyars, nor your courtiers to do so. And you are not to set up villages in the Novgorod volosts, nor is your princess, nor are your boyars, nor your courtiers to do so, nor to buy them or accept them as a gift. And you are not to set up free settlements[1] in the Novgorod volosts. As to your villages on Novgorod land, prince, or your princess's, or your boyars', you are to give up those villages; and you shall take money for them from those who seek them, who ever has bought what; and the land of St Sophia [is to go] to Novgorod. As to the Dmitriev villages and free settlements which we have given to Andrei for his lifetime on oath, afterwards all that [goes] to Novgorod; and, prince, you are not to enter into that. And you are to give the right boundary according to the old boundary on oath, as it was under your father Yaroslav. And you are to ride to Ozvad, prince, to hunt animals in summer. You are not to go to Rusa, only every third winter. And you are to go to Ladoga, prince, every third summer. And your sturgeon fisher is to go to Ladoga in accordance with your father's charter, as has been the custom. And you are not to hold a servant in Vologda. And your justices are to go through the volosts, where it has been the custom, in summer from St Peter's day,[2] in accordance with custom. As to the prince's meadows, those are the prince's; and what is Novgorod's is Novgorod's. And you are not to have the right to exile anyone in all the volosts of Novgorod. And from Suzdal' land, prince, you are not to judge a Novgorod man, nor to grant deeds, nor distribute volosts. And throughout Suzdal' land the Novgorod trader is to trade without restraint. And the customs due from a Novgorod and a Novy Torg trader is two vekshas[3] a load and a boat and a box of hops and of flax. And your courtiers are to receive according to custom; five kunas

---

[1] Free settlements were those, often established near borders or in sparsely settled areas, which were freed from payment of the main taxes as a means of attracting people to settle.　　　　　[2] 29 June.

[3] A small unit of money. In Smolensk it was $\frac{1}{24}$ of a nogata, $\frac{1}{480}$ of a grivna.

from the prince and two kunas from the servant. And beyond Volok, prince, you are not to send your man, you are to entrust your tribute to a Novgorod man. The word of a villein and a female slave is not to be taken against a master. And in the German establishment you, prince, are to trade through our fraternity; and you are not to appoint ushers, nor are you to close down an establishment. As to what has till now been done between you and your men to Novgorod prior to the oath, you, prince, and your men are to put it all aside. And your justices throughout the volosts are not of themselves to administer justice to the people throughout the Novgorod volosts. And the duel fee has not been customary throughout the Novgorod volosts, so your judges are to put it aside. And the slave and crop-sharer are not to be judged by your judges without their master; the prince is to judge in Novgorod as has been the custom. And the merchants are not to be judged in the volost arbitrarily. And whoever lives in Torzhok, on Novy Torg land, and is not subject to the Holy Saviour, [is subject] to Torzhok, [and] may be taken away by the prince, and you are to let them go from Torzhok wherever they will. But if a false accusation is brought to you, prince, against a man, you are not to give credence to it, but give him justice. And from the merchants you are not to have means of transport, unless there is news of war [to be carried]. And when, prince, you ride to Novgorod, then you are to have a gift as usual: but when you ride from Novgorod, then you have no need of a gift. If a villein or share-cropper flees to Tver' volost, you, prince, are to hand him over; if anyone asks for his case to be heard, let him be heard in Novgorod. And, prince, you are to put aside any disfavour towards the elders, the juniors and all. To all this, lord, kiss the cross in the presence of our brethren, the ambassadors.

6

This birch bark letter was found in spoil from a trench cut for sewage pipes near one of the excavations. It is, therefore, dated only by palaeography. It is of interest as the earliest evidence of peasants in Russia attempting themselves to define their obligations, doubtless as a means of forestalling any further increase in impositions on them. The rent in kind is distinguished from the gift; the former is similar to the 'income' item in the inquisitions of later date [see 38] while the latter and the final list of items resembles the item 'petty income'. Although the individuals here are siblings, this is not necessarily evidence that they farmed as a family.

Fourteenth century. Novgorod birch bark letter no. 136

NG (1953–4)

Now Mysl's children have agreed to give a rent in kind to Trufalya and his brothers, 6 measures[1] of rye and one of wheat, 3 of malt; the gift is 3 martens and a pud of honey; the children [are to give] each 3 squirrels[2] and 3 bundles of flax, a sheep and canvas.

[1] A measure (*korob'ya*, literally a 'basket' or 'bin') was a unit of volume. In the second half of the sixteenth century it amounted roughly to four bushels, but in this document we have the 'old' measure details of which do not appear to be known, although Nikitskii considered it was larger than the new one (*Zh MNP*, 1894, April, p. 379). Artsikhovskii merely comments on this birch bark letter that the unit is 'continually encountered in the Novgorod registers of inquisition' (*NG (1953–4)*, p. 78).

[2] The 'martens' (*kunnitsi*) and the 'squirrels' (*belki*) may have been units of money, not pelts.

37

7

Here a group of peasants ('orphans' is a common term for them on estates [see 9, 18]) complain to their lords about a steward. The sense of justice of the peasants comes through clearly, despite certain obscurities in the letter. The peasants expect the steward to stand up for them, not to sell their goods, presumably, nor plunder them; and they expect to be allowed to go off, probably to sell produce, or work for a period, off the estate. They hint at leaving the estate if the steward is not replaced.

The tree ring date of the layer in which this letter was found is 1369.

Second half of fourteenth century. Novgorod birch bark letter no. 370   NG (*1958–61*)

Greetings to Yuri and Maksim from all the orphans. The one you gave us as steward does not take our part, he sells us and we are plundered by him. We are stuck fast because of him, he does not let us go off. So we are lost. If he continues to be settled here, we have no strength to continue to be settled here. Give us a mild man. We beseech you for that.

8

The peasants writing this letter appeal to a lord for him to alter a decision. It is indicative of a strong sense of their rights that they feel able to question their lord's gift to another landlord. The gift, of course, cannot have been outright or the peasants would have had no grounds to appeal to the former lord; this suggests that Klim Oparin may have been a vassal of Mikhail Yurevich.

38

Late fourteenth century. Novgorod birch bark letter no. 311

To their [lord] Mikhail Yurevi[ch] your Cherenshani peasants[1]
petition you about the fact that you gave the little hamlet to
Klim Oparin. But we do not want him. He is not a neighbour
man. For he acts wilfully.

9

Here we have a very full picture of peasant obligations on a monastic
estate in the late fourteenth century. The peasants are not regarded
as a homogeneous group. There are the 'big people' who, in addition
to labour services performed with their own draught animals, have to
perform certain others not requiring draught animals; the 'horseless
peasants', from whom they are evidently distinguished, are obliged
mainly to process the raw materials produced (cp. Fr. *laboureurs* and
manouvriers). The causes of such peasant differentiation are obscure;
so also is the problem of how far obligations were in the form of
labour services or money payments. The term 'people' (*lyudi*) seems
frequently to have been used to indicate dependants, so that often it
referred to peasants, as in the last sentence of the body of this charter.
Peasant resistance to an alleged increase in obligations was the cause
of this attempt to draw up a custumal on this estate.

[1] Probably those from Cherenchitsy, see A. A. Konovalov in *SA* (1967), no. 1,
p. 88.

21 October 1391. Charter of Metropolitan Kiprian to the Emperor Constantine Monastery, Vladimir

AFZ i Kh, I, no. 201

Now I, Kiprian, Metropolitan of All Rus', have given this deed to the Saint Constantine Monastery and to the abbot. The monastery orphans complained to me against Efrem the abbot, saying; he imposes on us, lord, things not as of old, such as used not to be under the first abbots; he takes from us, lord, customary dues which other abbots did not have. And the abbot said thus to the Metropolitan: I, lord, am going according to the old custom as it was under the first abbots, and here, lord, in Moscow is Abbot Tsarko who was abbot at Saint Constantine before me, ask him, lord. And the Metropolitan sent Okinf to the Abbot Tsarko, since Tsarko was then ill, and ordered him to ask what was the custom in Saint Constantine's and how do the monastery people do their work? And Abbot Tsarko answered Okinf thus: thus it was in my abbacy in Saint Constantine the big people from the villages of the monastery had to put the church in order, to fence in the monastery and its courtyard, to put up buildings, compulsorily [*vzgonom*] to till the whole portion of the abbot's demesne arable; to sow, to reap, and to carry; to mow hay by desyatinas[1] and bring it into the yard; to make weirs in both spring and winter; to fence the orchards with wattle; to man the seine nets, to make ponds, to hunt beaver in autumn, to block up the springs; and at Easter and St Peter's[2] they each come to the abbot with something in their hands; and the horseless peasants from the villages thresh rye for the feast day and bake bread, grind malt, brew beer, thresh rye for seed; and the abbot gives flax to the villages and they weave nets [*sezhe*] and arrange the parts of the seines; and all the people from the

---

[1] A desyatina (*lit.* a tenth) was 2·7 acres.　　　[2] 29 June.

villages on the feast day give a heifer, but once they besought me, lord, but not according to custom, with three sheep, and I excused them the heifer as I had no need of the heifer, but according to the old custom there is always a heifer on the feastday; and if the abbot rides into any village for a celebration feast, the hopper men give each a basket of oats to the abbot's horses. And Okinf told all these speeches of Abbot Tsarko to the Metropolitan. And afterwards Abbot Tsarko recovered and came to the Metropolitan himself and told all these things that he had conveyed by Okinf to the Metropolitan. And afterwards I, Kiprian, Metropolitan of All Rus', questioned in Vladimir my boyars Mikhail Bireev, Yuri Protopopin and Ivan my cook, of the custom of that monastery and of the festival heifer [payment], and they told me the same things, both of the lakes and the springs and the beaver hunt. And Kiprian, Metropolitan of All Russia, said thus to the abbot and the monastery peasants: all of you follow my charter, the abbot is to maintain the orphans, and the orphans are to obey the abbot and to do the monastery work. And if there shall be any other abbot after this abbot, he too shall follow this my charter. And I have ordered this charter to be placed in the church for the abbot and the people, and no abbot shall carry this charter from the monastery; if he does, he shall have neither God's mercy, nor my blessing.

This charter was granted at Moscow in the year 6900 on the 21st day of October, indict 15.

[On the reverse, the signature:] the Grand Prince ordered this charter not to be violated and granted the abbot privilege according to this charter and what is written in it. And the Grand Prince's clerk, Ivan, signed. My, the Grand Prince's, fishermen are not to enter the monastery's lake.

Iona, Metropolitan of All Rus', has not violated this charter. But he has ordered the abbot and the peasants to go in everything according to the old custom and this charter. And in accordance with the Metropolitan's word, the Metropolitan's clerk, Karlo, signed.

41

IO

This charter was used as a model for subsequent ones; hence the phrase 'of the said name' in the text. It grants certain immunities to the Metropolitan, the head of the Orthodox Church in Russia at that time, and in general delimits the competence of the Metropolitan and the Grand Prince. In article 1, for instance, an attempt is made to prevent the dismemberment of the Church's holdings by sales to nobles or servitors. This article is also of interest in that it shows that custom was the basis for validating at least some obligations; if an obligation proved to be 'not according to custom' it might be cancelled. The Prince is concerned (articles 2, 3 and 9) to retain his right to sums due to the Tatars.

Article 4 is of particular interest. The 'people' [cp. 4, 9] of the Metropolitan who live in Moscow are to be registered. The making of inquisitions in order to compile registers was one of the characteristic steps which contributed to subsequent attempts to increase control over the peasantry [see also 13, 14, 20, 24, 28]. Again, article 12 shows the Prince's concern to maintain the number of his tribute-paying population and also gives an interesting criterion for deciding whether a priest's son is to be subject to the Metropolitan or the Prince [cp. 46].

28 June 1404. Charter agreed between the Grand Prince Vasilii Dimitrievich and the Metropolitan Kiprian, a contract between the Grand Prince and the Metropolitan about people and about church volosts[1]   PRP, III, 421–3

Now I, the Grand Prince of the said name, having consulted with my father of the said name, the Metropolitan of Kiev and All Rus', have issued rules about church houses and volosts, lands and waters, and about all customary church dues.

[1] Volost is evidently here used in the sense of 'estate'. See also [13].

1. The Metropolitan is to judge Lukhovets with its volost head or with the court investigator, but my, the Grand Prince's, justice is not to be [there]. And boyars and servitors of the Grand Prince and of the Metropolitan are not to buy Lukhovets lands; but if any shall have bought them, let them go off and take their money. And I, the Grand Prince, am to have tributes from Lukha for the general tax [for the Horde[1]] according to my deed relating to dues; [I am] not to have other than those dues; and the Grand Prince is to have neither tax nor impost [*belki, ni rezanki*], but the Metropolitan [is to have them]. And whereas the Lukhovets people used to build houses at the Grand Prince's court at Vladimir, that matter has been otherwise investigated [and it has been shown] that that was newly instigated and not according to custom, and now there is no need for the Lukhovets people to build houses at the Grand Prince's court.

2. But Seneg is his as has been gone into and established ot old: what is the Grand Prince's is the Grand Prince's, what is of the church, the Metropolitan's, is the Metropolitan's. And [I am] to have tribute from Seneg as general tax [for the Horde] according to my, the Grand Prince's, deed relating to dues, but [I am] not to have other than those dues.

3. As to the Metropolitan's church villages of our father which were long ago given even before Metropolitan Oleksei, those villages are subject to the Metropolitan as they were under Metropolitan Oleksei, and my, the Grand Prince's tribute collector and tax man[2] shall not be in those villages, but [I am] to have tribute from those villages for general tax [for the Horde] according to my, the Grand Prince's, dues deed, but [I am] not

---

[1] The Golden Horde was the name of that part of the Mongol Empire which dominated Russia from the early thirteenth to late in the fifteenth century.

[2] Possibly this term (*belshchik*) might mean an officer of the inquisition receiving a local payment, the census tax (*pischaya belka*). Cp. *belki* mentioned in [6], p. 37 n. 2. The phrase *belki, ni rezanki* in paragraph 1 also reminds us that both *belka* and *rezanka* were monetary units.

to have other than those dues; and the post-horse due,[1] as of old, every sixth day, and when my, the Grand Prince's, villages give [it], then the Metropolitan's give [it] too.

4. As to the Metropolitan's people who live in the town and are subject to the palace, they are to be registered and rent duties imposed on them as on my, the Grand Prince's, people who live in the town.[2]

5. And Constantine Monastery is eternally the Metropolitan's with its villages; and also Boris and Gleb Monastery with its villages; as they were subject from of old, even under Metropolitan Oleksei, thus they are also subject now.

6. As to the customary monastery villages, I, the Grand Prince, am not to send into those villages, nor judge them: let the abbots have cognisance of them and judge; if there is a joint court,[3] then the profit is half and half.

7. But if any man of mine, the Grand Prince's, takes suit against the abbot, or a priest or a monk, then [there is] a joint court; but if the Metropolitan shall chance not to be in my principality, if he rides far off into his metropolitanate, and someone beseeches me against a person of the Metropolitan, then, I, the Grand Prince, am to judge; if there is a joint court, then the profit is half and half; but if there is a Metropolitan's court, then the Metropolitan's representative judges. And also if anyone beseeches me, the Grand Prince, against the Metropolitan's representative, or against the tithe-collector[4] or the volost head, I, the Grand Prince, am to judge myself.

8. And the Metropolitan's church people are not to give goods tax, as it was also under Metropolitan Aleksei: whoever sells

---

[1] The due for the maintenance of the post-horse system was at this time probably not paid in money.

[2] If *dvorchan* is interpreted as suggested in *PRP*, IV, 434, this phrase should read 'people subject to the royal court official'.

[3] That is a court dealing with a case involving the Metropolitan's and the Prince's authority, for example, when dependants of both were involved.

[4] By this time the tithe-collector (*desyatinnik*) was a justice, rather than a collector of tithes.

his domestic stuff, he does not give the goods tax; but whoever has bought in stuff with which to trade, he gives goods
tax.

9. And when tribute is to be given to the Tatars, then also
the church people are to give dues; but when tribute is not to
be given to the Tatars, then also the church people are not to
give dues; and from Lukha the same.

10. As regards war, when I myself, the Grand Prince, mount
my horse, then also [shall] the Metropolitan's boyars and servitors, and [be] under the Metropolitan's military commander,
and under my, the Grand Prince's, banner; but if there is any
boyar or servitor who did not give service to the Metropolitan
Aleksei, but has newly put himself at the disposal of the Metropolitan, they go under my, the Grand Prince's, military commander; where each one lives, he is then under that military
commander.

11. And the Metropolitan is to have from the church six
altyns[1] of the payment to the church and three dengas of the
arrival fee, but apart from that he has no need of anything; and
the tithe-collector on taking up his office is to have as entry fee,
and as the Christmas gift and as the St Peter's day[2] gift, six
altyns, and apart from that he has no need of anything; and the
payment to the church is to be had at Christmas, and the
tithe-collector is to have his customary due at St Peter's day;
but whatever cathedral churches throughout the towns used
not to give payment to the church under the Metropolitan
Fegnost and Metropolitan Aleksei, they are not to give it now
either.

12. And the Metropolitan is not to appoint my, the Grand
Prince's, servitors and my tribute paying people as deacons or
priests. But if any priest's son, though he is registered in my
service, wants to become a priest or a deacon, then he is free
to do so. And a priest's son who lives with his father and eats
his father's bread, he is the Metropolitan's. But if any priest's

---

[1] An altyn was six dengas.   [2] 29 June.

son is separated and lives apart from his father and eats his own bread, he is mine, the Grand Prince's.

And the deed was written in Moscow, the 28th day of June, indict 12, the year 6900 [read: 6912 (1404)].

I I

In the period after the recovery from the impact of the Mongol invasions of the early thirteenth century, settlement of the forests seems to have taken place at an increased rate. It is extremely difficult to determine the scale of this movement, but we find many documents relating to the purchase of land, as here. Many others record gifts of land usually to monasteries. This evidence suggesting an increase in land deals is further strengthened by the references in many such documents to wastes (*pustoshi*). These were areas in the forest which had been cultivated; they were, therefore, of particular value because the initial work of clearance had been done. Such lands had subsequently either been abandoned, perhaps being used for hay or rough grazing, or had continued in cultivation but without any dwelling being built on the spot [see also 15]. It is not clear to what extent this evidence of resettlement and colonisation indicates an absolute growth of population above former levels.

This purchase deed records one estate near Tver bought from a well-known Novgorod boyar, with its village, dependent hamlets and their outlying wastes. Clearly the estate is well established. The bounds are marked by recognised arable and meadow and the area is administered by the owner's steward. At this period there seems to have been some increase in the attention paid to defining bounds in such documents; sometimes, however, bounds are indicated only by an indication of customary land use [see 15].

About 1380–1417. Purchase deed of Mikhail Fedorovich and his son Ivan relating to Medna village and its hamlets, Novy Torg uezd, bought from the Novgorod noble Yuri Ontsiforov

ASEI, I, no. 2

Mikhail Fedorovich and his son Ivan have bought from Yuri son of Ontsifor the village of Medna with the hamlets and wastes of old relating to Medna with all appurtenances and forest, and the meadow beyond the river Tvertsa along the bank near the Istar hayfields. And the bound and limit of that meadow is by its old gully from the river Tvertsa upstream, and from the gully by the hollow to the rock, and up the hollow opposite the three graves along Vyshny grave and straight to the river Tvertsa, and along the Tvertsa down by the Starsky arable and passing the Medna meadow goes straight to the Tvertsa. And they gave for Medna village with the hamlets, wastes and forest and every appurtenance and the meadow beyond the Tvertsa ninety Novgorod rubles.

And the witnesses are the good men: Mosi Alekseevich and Yakov Alekseevich, and Vasili son of Ivan and Yuri son of Olfim.

And whoever shall enter a claim to that land, the steward shall clear the land [of those claims]...And I shall settle with whoever enters claims to that land before God on the day of judgement.

And Yakov Bobrovnikov wrote the purchase deed.

12

This document gives us evidence of peasant movement, apparently without any particular limitations, in an early fifteenth century Novgorod estate; the tree ring dates are 1409 and 1422. Two peasants had been huntsmen and also peasants of the town head; at some stage, it is not entirely clear when, they had been dependants of Aleksei Shchuka (literally 'Pike'), probably a lesser lord.

Early fifteenth century. Novgorod birch bark letter no. 310

NG (1956–7)

Petition to the lord, Andrei Ivanovich, town head of Novgorod, from your steward, Vavula, and from your peasants, the peasants which came to you from being huntsmen, Zakharka and Nesterka lived with Aleksei Shchuka. Now, lord, Aleksei does not want to give us rye. As this is so, lord, show favour to us, your peasants. We rely, lord, on God and on you, on our lord.

13

In the early fifteenth century, we find the first evidence of the registration of dependants on the estates as a result of inquisitions [see 10]. Here we have the first such instance attested on country estates of the royal family. It is, of course, quite probable that such registration may have been carried out earlier, but we have no knowledge of it. In these early inquisitions it is noteworthy that people pay 'according to their ability' [cp. 18]; later, the clerks of the inquisition made a tax assessment for each tenement.

In the second paragraph of this brief extract, the sentence starting 'But if God changes the Horde' refers to what is to happen if the domination of the Golden Horde, the Tatar-Mongol overlord, ceases to be effective.

On the date of this will see A. A. Zimin, *PI*, VI, 293–4, 323.

March 1423 (possibly earlier; the earliest date possible being 1419). Extract from the (Third) will of the Grand Prince Vasilii Dmitrievich D i DG, no. 22

And from Novgorod half of all my customary dues to my princess. And as to any village I have given her in Novgorod or any acquisition, that is hers. And Sokol'skoe village is hers with everything [that is subject to it]. And Kerzhanets with all is my princess's. And from Murom, Seltse and Shatur to my princess.

My son and my princess shall send and make an inquisition, and impose tribute on the people according to their ability to pay in those volosts and villages which I have given to my princess, and my princess shall give tribute from those volosts and villages according to the reckoning and the post-horse due, whenever it is to be had from them. But if God changes the Horde, then my princess shall take that tribute to herself and my son, the prince Vasilii, is not to interfere. And she judges herself her volost heads and servants and court investigators, but my son, prince Vasilii, is not to send into her volosts or her villages for any reason at all. And these volosts and villages are to be my princess's for her lifetime, apart from Gzhelya and Semtsinskoe village and her additions by purchase and acquisitions, and on her death [they go] to my son, prince Vasilii. And in Gzhelya and in Semtsinskoe village and its acquisitions my princess is free, let her give it to whomever she wishes. And if any boyar serves my princess, my son, prince Vasilii, shall look after those boyars of hers.

14

This grant illustrates a characteristic development in the fifteenth century. Recuperation from the Mongol invasions involved both settlement of the forests and increased attention to land as the basis of wealth and power; this, in its turn, resulted in attempts at closer control of the estate population. We have already noted the first documentary evidence for the registration of dependants [10, 13]. At the same time as this demand for labour was being experienced the principality of Moscow was on the way to establishing its predominance over the other Russian principalities. The fragmentation of the land between a number of principalities was giving way to its unification. It was in these circumstances that this grant was made. In it the Grand Prince offers freedom from a range of obligations, including tribute, and apparently without term, for peasants ('people') whom the monastery can succeed in attracting from other areas, as long as they are not subject to the Grand Prince's jurisdiction. These newcomers ('arrivals') are now distinguished from the old-established peasants, those already living on the estate and, perhaps, even registered there, though these terms are probably of general, rather than narrowly juridical significance.

2 June 1425. A royal grant by the Grand Prince Vasilii Vasil'evich to Abbot Nikon of the Trinity Monastery to Beklemishevo and hamlets   ASEI, I, no. 44

For the sake of the Holy Trinity, in accordance with the deed of my father, the Grand Prince Vasilii Dmitrievich, I, the Grand Prince Vasilii Vasilevich, have granted the Abbot Nikon and the brethren, or whatever other abbot there shall be after him a privilege. As regards their villages in Kinela stan,[1] of Bek-

---

[1] Stan is an administrative subdivision of a volost [see 10]. Note that 'villages' is here used in the general sense of 'lands'.

lemishevo, Vyakhoreva hamlet, Nozar'eva hamlet, Faustovo waste, Voronino, Bunkovo, Olfer'evo and whatever people live in those villages, and hamlets and wastes, the Kinela volost heads and their servants are not to send to them for any reason, nor to judge them, apart from cases of murder; the Abbot Nikon, or whomever he orders, is to have cognisance of them and judge them. If there is a joint court, the volost heads and their servants judge and the Abbot Nikon, or whomever he orders, judges his. Whether a monastery man is right or guilty the Abbot deals with him in right and in guilt, but the volost officers and their servants are not to enter [claims] for any reason against those people who live in those villages. Whether a volost man is right or guilty, the volost officer or his servant has cognisance of him in right and in guilt, and the Abbot is not to enter [claims] against a volost man, neither right nor guilty for any reason. And if anyone shall call people from other principalities and not from my Grand Principality's estate to those villages, hamlets and wastes, I have no need of my Grand Prince's tribute from those people who have come, nor of the census tax, nor of the post-horse due, nor of the provision of horses, nor of making defences, nor of any other customary dues, nor of communal obligations, nor of contribution, nor of any commune payment. Nor is there need [of any obligations] upon those people who are arrivals or upon the old-established peasants to feed my horse, to mow my hay, nor of the fodder due, nor the mowing tax,[1] nor tailoring, nor are they to owe anything to the steward or the hundred-man or the stan official.

And whoever contrary to this deed of mine takes anything of them or offends in any way shall be penalised.

And the deed was granted at Moscow, the second day of June in the year six thousand nine hundred and thirty-three.

[1] The fodder due and the mowing tax appear to be possible commutations of the obligations 'to feed my horse, to mow my hay' mentioned immediately preceding.

15

This purchase deed is of interest because there is other documentary evidence which suggests that Protas Chernobesov was a peasant. If so, we here have evidence for peasant ownership of a heritable estate and for peasant literacy. Gilevo waste is later recorded as a hamlet and thus illustrates that process of winning land from the forest already touched on in [11].

Not later than 1438–40. Purchase deed of Ivan Kuzmin for Gilevo and Semenikovo wastes, Nerekhta volost, Kostroma uezd,[1] bought of Protas Martynov Chernobesov

ASEI, I, no. 137

Now, I, Ivan Kuzmin, have bought of Protas Martynov Chernobesov the waste of Gilevo, his heritable estate, and Semenikovo waste with all that appertains to those wastes, wherever the plough, the axe and the scythe have been,[2] apart from the Medvezhenka hay-fields. And I have given four rubles for them, and a cow as fulfilment.[3]

And the witnesses of that [deed]: Aleksandr Alfer'evich Lapot and Elizar Yur'evich, and Ivan Davydev, and Gregory Vasil'ev Goryshkin.

And Protas himself wrote the purchase deed in his own hand. And the deed is without a seal.

[1] An uezd was an administrative area, sometimes, as here, headed by a town and divided into volosts.

[2] This was a common formula used in documents of the fourteenth to fifteenth centuries and may be taken to indicate the customary boundaries of arable, meadow and forest, i.e. the three essential elements of any farm or settlement. Cp. [17, 19], etc.

[3] When contracts were agreed some fairly small gift was made in addition to the price specified. This has been regarded by some commentators as an archaic survival from a time when there were no purchases only exchanges.

16

This birch bark letter, possibly from the 1420s, records the reaction of peasants on a Novgorod estate of a great noble to excessive impositions. Half have already fled and, according to the estate servant writing, the other half wish to go.

First half of the fifteenth century. Novgorod birch bark letter no. 301   NG (1956–7)

To the lord Mikhail Yurevich, the town head's son, your follower Klya greets you. How, lord, will you pity the estate? Half is empty and those who have remained wish to go. They wish to complain, lord, complain so that, lord, the dues should be reduced. And I greet you, my lord.

17

Like [14], this immunity frees both old-established peasants and newcomers from other principalities from certain obligations. Again, the references to wastes and the inclusion of a free settlement remind us of the processes of forest clearance, settlement and the attempts to attract hands continually taking place in this period. The granting of the estate itself as a gift was evidently due to the debt of twenty Novgorod and ten current (Moscow) rubles.

1432–45. Immunity of Princess Agrafena of Sheksna, widow of Prince Afanasii Ivanovich, and her children, Semen and Vasilii

ASEI, I, no. 103

Now, I, Princess Agrafena [widow] of Prince Afanasii Ivanovich with my children Prince Semen and Prince Vasilii Afanasevich have given to the Holy Trinity Monastery of St Sergius, to the Abbot Zinovei and the brethren, or any other abbot there shall be after him, in our estate on the Sheksna the little St Nikola monastery with the Nikola land and hayfields and forest down the Sheksna along by Krinichishche and up along the Sheksna by Avakumovo land, and up by the Sheksna [we have given] the Goluzino waste and Nakhta[1] and the little free settlement in Sosnyaga and Rogatski and Divnovo and Melkoshino and Elyakovo and Barmino and Berezovo. And we have given those wastes with all that, wherever the plough, the sokha and the scythe have been. And the boundary of those lands is from the estate of Prince Ivan Andreevich along the river Pushma.

And on the other side of the Sheksna we have given Chevskoe, also with its hayfields and forest and with all that appertains to it. And we have given the Berezovo weir on the river Sheksna and two nights on the Vyachevo weir[2] of Nikola and the Ustenski weir on the Sheksna[3] which they can make where they will. And whatever monastery people they have, they are free to catch anything in the Sheksna and the Volga, we have no need of any due or justice; and they are to fish with two monastery seines both in the Volga and in the Sheksna, otherwise we have no need of any due on that from them; but if,

[1] A small tributary of the Sheksna.
[2] The catch from certain weirs was so prolific that rights were granted in terms of a certain number of nights, or even half-nights.
[3] Instead of Ustenski being a place-name, it might mean 'at the mouth' of the Sheksna.

apart from these two seines, they start to fish with other seines for the monastery, we princes shall have a due as of old. And we have given this for our parents and ourselves to be remembered in the Holy Trinity. And as for the thirty rubles we had to give to the monk Aleksandr Rusan, twenty Novgorod rubles and ten current rubles,[1] our lord, the Trinity Abbot Zinovei and the brethren have taken that away from us. And whatever old-established peasants live at St Nikola's and whatever people they [i.e. the monastery authorities] call from other principalities to themselves, but not from our estate, to St Nikola and to all those wastes, or their monastery fishermen, we have no need of any due from those people nor have our dues-collectors. Nor shall we judge those monastery people, nor their fishermen, but their abbot, or whomever he orders, shall judge those people. And if there is a joint case between our people and monastery people, the abbot's official and our official shall judge jointly. And whether the monastery man is right or guilty he is dealt with by the abbot's official in right and in guilt, and our official shall not come for a monastery man, right or guilty. And whether our man is right or guilty he is subject to ours in right and in guilt, and the abbot's official shall not come in right or in guilt for our man. And the abbot's official shall not grant other fishermen from beyond the boundary freedom to fish, but only his own monastery people and fishers. If any case shall occur with a difference between the abbot's official and our official, then they shall have as third man Abbot Zinovei of the Trinity Monastery of St Sergius, or whatever abbot there shall be after him.

And the witnesses: Fedor Semenovich and Mikhail Afanas'-evich, and the monk Aleksandr Rusan, and the monk Benjamin Skripitsin.

And the priest John wrote the deed.

[1] At this period there existed two rubles: the 'Novgorod' ruble of 216 dengas and the 'current' or 'Moscow' ruble of 200 dengas.

18

Here we have a rather vague grant of immunity. Despite the imposing opening, no detailed list of the villages concerned is given. The general provisions, however, are similar to those in other immunities, but, unlike the ones we have had so far, the exemption from obligations for newcomers from other principalities is here limited to a period of ten years.

April 1435. Confirmation of a grant of immunity by the Grand Prince Vasilii Vasil'evich to Mikhail Yakovlevich and his children in right of his heritable estates in Kinela volost and Gorodskoi [i.e. the town] stan, Pereyaslavl' uezd

ASEI, I, no. 117

Now I, the Grand Prince Vasilii Vasil'evich, in accordance with my great-great-grandfather's, Grand Prince Ivan Danilovich's deed, and in accordance with the deed of my great-grandfather's brother, the Grand Prince Semen Ivanovich, and in accordance with my great-grandfather's, Grand Prince Ivan Ivanovich's deed, and in accordance with my grandfather's, Grand Prince Dmitrii Ivanovich's deed, and in accordance with my father's, Grand Prince Vasilii Dmitrievich's deed, have made a grant to Mikhail Yakovlich and his children. As to their villages in Kinela and in the town uezd, in Pereyaslavl', my Pereyaslavl' royal representatives and the Kinela volost heads and their servants are not to send in to them their court investigators for any reason, nor to their people, and are not to judge them apart from murder and theft discovered with the goods or brigandage also with the goods;[1] but they [i.e. Mikhail Yakovlevich and

---

[1] In many instances immunities excluded the most important crimes from the grant.

his children], or whomever they order to do so [on their behalf], are to judge their people themselves. If there is a joint court with the towns people or the volost people, both the royal representatives and the volost heads and their servants are to judge and Mikhail and his children, or whomever they order, judge with them; and the court tax is to be divided. And the royal court officials and the stan officials are not to send into those villages to their people for any reason, either for any service of mine, or for communal obligations, or for hay tax. And when my tribute comes [to be collected], those orphans,[1] too, pay my tribute according to their ability, apart from the stan people,[2] nor have they any need to pay the goods tax, nor the eighth tax, nor the customs due, nor the tax [*kostki*]; [they need pay] no customary dues; and when the post-horse due comes [to be collected], then they are to give that post-horse due to the town, apart from the stan officials. And whatever people they summon into those villages from other principalities, and not from my, the Grand Prince's, estate, those people who are arrivals have no need to pay any of my tribute, the post-horse due, or the census tax, or provision of horses, no customary dues for ten years and they are to be judged by the same Mikhail and his children or whomever they order [to judge on their behalf]. And when their term is up, those people are liable to pay my tribute according to their ability with their people, apart from the stan officials.

And whoever contrary to this deed offends them in anything or takes anything shall be penalised.

But sometimes I grant a charter which affects holders of privileges, but as regards this deed there is no other deed.

And the deed was granted at Moscow, April in the year 6000 and 900 and 43. [On the reverse:] Andrei Konstantinovich. [Below, a monogram].

---

[1] See [9] for the use of this term to indicate peasants on a monastic estate.
[2] The stan people are those under the jurisdiction not of private landlords, but of the prince's officials.

19

Land could be mortgaged in order to obtain a loan. In the document given here the produce of the land (the hay obtained from the waste) is to be taken for interest; this was quite a common procedure. Moreover, if the debt was not repaid on time the land was retained by the creditor. That this was a frequent occurrence is suggested by the fact that the deed is drawn up both as a mortgage note and as a deed of purchase. Sometimes, however, the mortgaging of land was simply a device to avoid family claims to repurchase any land sold. Land was regarded, in fact, not as being the exclusive property of the individual who held it, but rather as the property of the family, that is those who had a claim to its use. Disposal of it by sale was therefore subject to a right of pre-emption by other family members (cp. French *retrait lignager*). Cp. [29].

There is no mention of any labour force, probably because the waste was worked as an outlying area and had no house on it.

About 1447–55. Mortgage obligation of Vasyuk Noga Esipov to the monk of the Trinity Monastery of St Sergius, Gerontius Likharev, relating to Luka waste, Uglich uezd

ASEI, I, no. 216

Copy of an obligation to the Monk Gerontius.

Now I, Vasyuk Noga son of Esip, have taken from Gerontius, the monk of the Trinity Monastery of St Sergius, two rubles and a quarter in current Moscow money at five grivnas for a poltina[1] from Easter to the feast of St Dmitrius.[2] And for that money I have handed Gerontius my land, Luka waste, along the

---

[1] 1 Moscow ruble = 200 dengas: 1 grivna = 20 dengas; 1 poltina = 100 dengas.

[2] 11 February, the feast of Demetrius of the Luka area.

Kashin boundary with everything [appertaining to it], wherever the plough and the scythe and the axe have gone. And for interest Gerontius is to mow that Luka waste. And if I do not buy back that waste on time, on St Dmitrius's day, then for Gerontius this is my obligation and [his] deed of purchase for that land of mine.

And the witnesses were: Kazak Skrypitsin, Avram Byvaltsov, Grid'ya Puminov, and the monastery servant Myakhkoi.

And Fodko Golokhvastov wrote the deed.

And no verbal obligation[1] is to be made as regards this obligation without informing a senior official.

Postscript to the obligation: Appearing before Klimentii Grigorevich, Vasko Esipov Noga said that he had taken two rubles and a quarter from the Trinity monk Gerontius and given this obligation on himself. And he said that he had granted his Luka waste, along the Kashin boundary, to Gerontius for this money, as was written in this obligation. And Klimentii Grigorevich also appended his seal to this obligation. And the clerk Semen signed it.

20

This is another grant of immunity illustrating the concern of landlords to attract peasants by granting exemption from the obligations due to the Grand Prince. In the first case any 'people' who 'begin to live', i.e. begin to make a livelihood by working the land, are freed from certain such obligations (cp. a very similar phrase, though at a different social level, in [24]). Second, those who are 'arrivals', i.e. not old-established peasants, and are from other principalities are freed from customary dues for ten years [cp. 14]. The reservation is made, however, that the Prince's peasants, whether registered [see 13] or not, are not to be accepted as tenants by the monastery.

[1] If the interpretation of this term (*izustnaya*) suggested in *ASEI*, 1, 746 is correct, this phrase should read: 'And no bequest...'

17 March 1460. Grant of immunity by the Grand Prince Vasilii Vasil'evich to Afanasi, Archimandrite of Simonov Monastery

ASEI, II, no. 359

Now I, the Grand Prince Vasilii Vasil'evich, have made a grant to Afanasii, Archimandrite of Simonov Monastery, and the brethren, or whatever other archimandrite there shall be after him; Andrei Yarlyk gave them, the Simonov Monastery of the Immaculate Virgin, his manorial village Byl'tsino with its hamlet in Kisma, Pereyaslavl' volost, and, also in the Pereyaslavl' uezd, the hamlet Rozhestvenskaya and Abakumtsevo waste, and any people who begin to live under them, those people of theirs have no need to pay the post-horse due, nor make provision of horses, nor feed my horse, nor mow my hay; neither are they to be subject to the hundred-men nor the royal court officials for any reason, nor [to make] any commune payments nor to perform communal obligations; nor do they need to pay any other customary dues, nor to set up the tenement of the volost head at Kisma. And whatever people are summoned from Kashin, Tver [principality], to that manorial village and to the hamlets and the wastes, those people who are arrivals from other principalities have no need to pay my, the Grand Prince's, tribute, nor the post-horse due, nor provision of horses nor any other customary due for ten years. But they are not to accept my, the Grand Prince's, registered people and unregistered people. And the archimandrite himself is to have cognisance of and to judge his people, or whomever he orders; my Pereyaslavl' royal representatives and Kisma volost heads and their servants are not to send to them for anything, nor are they to take any of their living; and the court bailiffs and investigators are not to take their dues. Also my Pereyaslavl' royal representatives and Kisma volost heads and their servants are not to judge those their people for anything apart from manslaughter and brigandage and red-handed theft. And if there occurs a joint case of their people with the town people or with the volost ones, both my Pereyaslavl' royal representatives and Kisma volost heads and their servants judge, and the archimandrite's official judges with them; they divide the profits in half. And if there shall be any case against their official then I, the Grand Prince, shall judge him myself or my authorised boyar.

And if anyone offends them contrary to this my deed, let him be punished by me, the Grand Prince.

And the deed has been granted at Moscow in the year 6960 and eight, on the 17th day of March.

2 1

In this document the peasants of a volost make an agreement with one of the main Novgorod monasteries about the rents they are to pay and the customary dues to which they are liable. Five of their number act on behalf of 'all the Robychitsy peasants'. This is an unusual document, but it may be compared with [8]. In that birch bark letter a particular family, not a volost, made a similar agreement about their obligations.

About 1460. Agreement of the Robychitsy volost peasants with St George's Monastery concerning their obligations and gifts
                                                    GVN i P, no. 115

With the blessing of the most holy lord and sovereign Archbishop of Novgorod the Great and Pskov, Archbishop Iona. Now these peasants of Robychitsy made an agreement with Archimandrite Grigori and with the priests and monks of St George's Monastery: Fedor, Smen Onkudinov, Ovdotei Maksimov, Sofontii Vasil'ev, Petr Sidorov and all the Roby-

61

chitsy peasants. They are to give a rent in kind, 30 measures of rye, 30 of oats[1] in true Novgorod units to the granary. And they are themselves to cart that grain to the monastery of the Holy Saviour and St George. The estate bailiffs are to have the village due as of old. And if the archimandrite rides in on a progress he is to rest at the stopping place two nights and the peasants are to supply beer enough and bread and dainties, fish and meat enough, and enough oats and hay for the horses. And the gift to the archimandrite at that stopping place is 5 grivnas; the sewer has half a measure of rye, the cup-bearer has half a measure of rye, the priest and monk have a measure of rye, the deacon a quarter of rye, the cook and groom a measure of rye, the young men a measure of rye, the treasurer and carter a quarter of rye, the Novgorod court ushers half a measure of rye. But if the archimandrite does not come on his progress, then those paying the customary dues are not liable to any of them, but the peasants have to send the archimandrite's gift of 5 grivnas to the monastery. But if the peasants do not pay those rents in kind and those customary dues, then the archimandrite and the priests and monks shall deal with them according to the old deeds of the princes and those of Novgorod.

22

In this grant Vasilii II makes it clear that no one has the right to withdraw peasants or old-established peasants from part of the Trinity Monastery estate. This evidently refers to the activities of other land-lords or their estate officials in the search for additional peasants to settle on their lands. It thus looks as if the summoning of peasants from other estates had begun to reach a point of conflict in some areas and at some levels of society. Whether the first part of the document was included because the feasts and drinking were used as recruitment opportunities we do not know.

[1] See [6], p. 37 n. 1.

1455–62. Charter of privilege by the Grand Prince Vasilii Vasil'evich to Abbot Vasian of the Trinity Monastery of St Sergius

ASEI, I, no. 264

Now I, the Grand Prince Vasilii Vasil'evich, have made a grant to the Abbot Vasian of Trinity and the brethren, that as to their monastery's village Priseki in Bezhetsk Verkh, with its hamlets, the servants and court investigators of my Bezhetsk representatives, and also the boyar people, or anyone else uninvited, shall not go for beer to their monastery people, whoever may live under them in that village and the hamlets. But if anyone arrives uninvited at a feast to their man and some loss is caused, I have ordered that loss to be made good without trial and enquiry, and let him also be punished by me. I have also granted the abbot and brethren: that if anyone withdraws [and takes] to himself any peasant of theirs from that village and from the hamlets and their old-established peasant, I, the Grand Prince, have ordered them not to release those peasants from Priseki and the hamlets to anyone.

23

Here we have another grant by Vasilii II; this authorises the return of 'people' i.e. peasants, who have left the monastery's estate in order to avoid defence obligations at the river bank against Tatar inroads. The people who 'now live in their villages' are here treated in similar fashion to old-established peasants and those who have been registered on a particular estate; they have no right to move away, and if they do move away they are to be returned. If necessary, the monastic estate officials can seek help from the royal officers of justice in the county town.

1455–62. Charter of privilege by the Grand Prince Vasilii Vasil'evich to Abbot Vasian of the Trinity Monastery of St Sergius on the removal of peasants   ASEI, I, no. 265

Now I, the Grand Prince Vasilii Vasil'evich, have made a grant to the Abbot Vasian of the Trinity Monastery and the brethren. As to their villages in Uglich uezd and any people who have left them from those villages and [gone] to my, the Grand Prince's, villages or the villages of my Grand Princess, and to boyar villages this year, not wishing to go on my, the Grand Prince's, service to the river bank, I, the Grand Prince, have granted a privilege to the Abbot Vasian and the brethren and ordered those people to be removed back again. But whatever people now live in their villages, I, the Grand Prince, have ordered them not to let those people go. If the monastery's village overseer needs an usher, he shall take an usher from my royal representative at Uglich against those people who have left them.

24

This is a short extract from the will of Vasilii II. The bulk of the document disposes his estate to his sons, but a quite considerable part of the main will is concerned with bequests to his wife. This part shows how provision was made for surveys to be carried out on the royal estates in order to assess liability to the general tax to be paid to the Golden Horde. We have already seen that making inquisitions and registering peasants on estates was a preliminary step to restricting their right to move [see 10, 13, 20 above and also 28 below]. A brief extract from one such inquisition of later date is given in [38].

3 May 1461–27 March 1462. Extract from the will of the Grand Prince Vasilii Vasil'evich   D i DG, no. 61, p. 197

And I give my princess half of all my customary dues from Nizhni Novgorod, as it was with my mother, the Grand Princess, and also the villages which were my mother's, the Grand Princess's, together with all customary dues and whatever [services] were liable to be rendered to them and with Sokolovskoe village and with Kerzhenets. And I give my princess from Murom the manorial village of Muromskoe and Shatur and my children are not to interfere there.

And when my children begin to live in their portions,[1] my princess and my son Ivan and my son Yuri and my children shall send their clerks of inquisition and these clerks shall record their portions on oath, and in accordance with that register they shall tax by sokha-units and people and in accordance with that prescription my princess and my children shall begin to give my son Ivan general tax for the Horde from their portions. But if God changes the Horde, my princess and my children shall take to themselves the tribute from their portions and my son Ivan shall not interfere in that.

25

In the fifteenth century, and particularly late in that century, money played an increasingly important part in the countryside. A key term reflecting this is 'silver' (*serebro*). It has a number of meanings which it is not always possible to distinguish clearly. Sometimes, like French *argent*, it means money, but it never became the established word for money. Usually it indicates rents or loan repayments

---

[1] I.e. begin to extract income from these estates. At peasant level the phrase 'begin to live' meant to begin to make a livelihood directly from the land [see 20].

in money; it can also mean simply income in money. The interest on loans was not always paid in money, however, but was sometimes worked off and thus approximated to labour rent. Rent and repayment were indeed often not sharply differentiated; to the lord at that time both were income. Moreover, the peasant debt might be due not to a loan, but to the accumulation of rent arrears. In this document, then, the silver-men are peasants owing money to the monastery either as rent or as loan repayments.

Share-croppers (*polovniki*, literally 'halvers', a term commoner in the Novgorod lands than in the central areas) were a category of peasants who paid a stipulated proportion of their harvest as rent. They have already been mentioned in [5]. In this document the share-cropper (halver) silver-men could be indebted peasants paying half (or some other share) of their harvest as interest, but they might be those paying a money rent to the value of a fixed proportion of their harvest.

The document shows that the Prince was forced to make a concession to the monastery. Peasants are only to move away from the monastery estate at one period in the year, in very late autumn; such peasants are only to move if they have paid their debts or found sureties and the concession of a terminable privilege (see p. 67 n. 2) is withdrawn. The movement of peasants away from the estate was probably connected with an increase in labour services arising from the fact that the monastery had obtained in 1450 the right to portage dues on a third of all vessels using the portage with the river Onega on the White Sea–Vologda trade route. This was a source of considerable income.

1455–67. Deed and reading by Prince Mikhail Andreevich of Vereya and Beloozero to Fedor Kontstantinovich [Monastyrev], the volost head of Volochek Slovenskii, on accepting [removal of] silver-men peasants from the Therapontis hermitage at one date a year, at the autumn St George's day,[1] on payment by them of the silver to the monastery

ASEI, II, no. 326

[1] 26 November.

From Prince Mikhail Andreevich to Fedor Konstantinovich. The Abbot Ekim and the monk Martemyan and all the brethren of the Therapontis hermitage sent the monk Eustrati to me and petitioned and said that the Volochek reeve showed them my deed which said that they [the volost authorities] were to accept the monastery's share-croppers on silver to themselves to your section,[1] the Volochek volost, from Martemyan's hamlets in the middle of the summer and at all times; and if any share-cropper silver-man, it says, should go out into your section, then he is to pay the capital in two years without interest.[2] And I have granted a privilege to the Abbot Ekim and the monk Martemyan and all the brethren, and you should not accept monastic people, silver-men from St George's day to St George's day; but you should accept silver-men at the autumn St George's day; but if any monastic people go at St George's day into your section, then they shall pay the money; and I have annulled that terminable privilege. And I have ordered the abbot and all the brethren not to release the silver-men from their hamlets from St George's day to St George's day, but I have ordered them to release the silver-men two weeks before St George's day and a week after St George's day. But if any come out into your section [who are] on monastery silver and they have been working off that silver, they should give sureties on the silver; and when autumn comes, then they should have paid off the silver. And after reading this deed through, give it back to the Abbot Ekim and the monk Martemyan and all the brethren.

[1] The 'section' (*put'*) refers either to the administrative area, in this case the volost, or to the area of competence of the official; here it probably has the former meaning.
[2] Debtors could appeal to the Prince for the grant of a terminable privilege [see 39] which authorised repayment of the capital sum of a debt over a stated number of years, but excused the debtor from paying interest.

5-2

26

This document, like [25], restricts the movement of share-croppers and silver-men to one period in the year. Previously in this area, there seem to have been two terminal dates each year, late in December and late in June. The 'people on contract' appear to be the same as the 'free settlement people', i.e., those attracted to the monastery by the establishment of free settlements where those settling were granted exemption from obligations, and this was evidently regarded as a form of contract (*ryad*), perhaps because the exemption was for a stipulated limited period.

1448–70. Deed of Prince Mikhail Andreevich of Vereya and Beloozero to Beloozero, to his representative, boyars, junior boyars, chamberlains and village overseers on forbidding withdrawal of silver-men, share-croppers and people on contract from the St Cyril of Beloozero Monastery other than at St George's day ASEI, II, no. 138

From Prince Mikhail Andreevich to Beloozero, to my representative and to all the boyars and junior boyars[1] and chamberlains and my village overseers, to all without exception. My father [confessor] the Abbot Kas'yan of St Cyril monastery petitioned me and says that you are withdrawing from him the monastery's silver-men and share-croppers and St George's [day] people on contract. And you withdraw them other than at St George's day, some at Christmas and others at St Peter's

---

[1] Fletcher in the sixteenth century called these 'the lowe pensioners'; they were petty service tenants and by this time did not necessarily have any direct boyar connection, though originally the Russian expression for them, 'boyar children', may have been literally true.

day.[1] And you should not withdraw silver-men and share-croppers and free settlement people. But the silver-men and the share-cropper is to be withdrawn at St George's day and is to pay the silver. But after St George's day there is no withdrawal for the silver-man. But if he pays the silver, then he may be withdrawn. And I have ordered the abbot not to let the silver-men go after St George's day. And whoever disobeys this my deed shall be punished by me.

27

Like [25] and [26] this deed restricts peasant movement to one period of the year. The estate of the Trinity Monastery was the largest in Russia and this, together with the fact that the document mentions 'people' in general, without limiting the restriction to certain categories, suggests that restrictions on peasant movement were then quite widespread. Nevertheless, the document specifically refers to only one village and its dependent hamlets.

1463–68. Deed and reading of the Grand Prince Ivan Vasil'evich to Yaroslavl', to the boyar and royal representative Prince Ivan Vasil'evich Obolenskii, on the petition of the Abbot of the Trinity Monastery of St Sergius about the with-drawal of monastic peasants from the village of Fedorovskoe only in the week before St George's day in the autumn and in the week after it   *ASEI*, I, no. 338

From the Grand Prince Ivan Vasil'evich to Yaroslavl', to my boyar and royal representative, Prince Ivan Vasil'evich, and in

[1] 29 June.

the volost to the volost heads and your servants and your officials. The Abbot of the Trinity Monastery of St Sergius and the brethren have petitioned me about the fact that, they say, people withdraw from them to my estate, to Yaroslavl', between St George's days from their village of Fedorovskoe, in Nerekhta [volost], and the hamlets. And I, the Grand Prince, have granted them a privilege: I have ordered them in Yaroslavl' not to release the people from their village of Fedorovskoe and the hamlets other than at St George's day. And should anyone of them withdraw other than at St George's day, I have ordered them to take him back. But you are not to withdraw those people of theirs from them between St George's days. But if anyone wishes to withdraw from them to my estate, to Yaroslavl', then you are to withdraw them from them at St George's day, a week before St George and a week after St George's day, for two weeks, But between St George's days you are not to withdraw anyone from them in accordance with this my deed.

And having read this my deed, give it them back and they will keep and preserve it.

28

The main interest in this document lies in its excluding 'any tribute paying people who are registered' from those granted exemption from obligations. Such peasants were not to be accepted as new-comers to the estate and this prohibition reinforced the attempt to limit peasant movement by registering the peasants. We have already seen a number of instances of registration of peasants on estates for tax and other purposes [10, 13, 20, 24].

15 January [1466]. Grant of immunity by the Grand Princess Mariya Yaroslavna to Stefanida, widow of Vas. Mikh. Shein

ASEI, I, no. 341

In accordance with the charter of my lord, the Grand Prince Vasilii Vasil'evich, I, the Grand Princess Mariya, have granted a privilege to Stefanida, wife of Vasilii Mikhailovich, and her son Dmitrii Vasil'evich, that their villages in Vol'skaya [volost], Ivanovskoe and Lavrent'evskoe, and Pogorelovo with its hamlets, and whatever people they have to live in their villages and hamlets, those people have no need to pay customs dues, nor goods tax nor the post-horse due nor provision of horses, nor to feed my horse, nor to mow my hay, nor to be subject to the hundred-men and the royal court officials nor the ten-men nor [to pay] any commune payments, nor communal obligations along with the subject[1] people; they have no need to pay any other customary dues. But they are not to accept into those villages and hamlets any tribute paying people who are registered. And the volost heads and their Vol'skaya servants are not to take their living from them, nor to send in to them for anything, nor to judge them in anything, apart from manslaughter and red-handed brigandage and theft. And the court bailiffs and investigators are not to take their dues from them, nor to ride in to them for anything. And Stefanida or her son Dmitri are to have cognisance of and to judge those their people. And if a joint case occurs for those their people and the volost people, the Vol'skaya volost heads [and] their servants shall judge, and Dmitrii shall judge with them, or whomever he orders; and they divide the court income in half. If anyone

---

[1] The term *tyagly* means 'liable to tax'. Society was divided, broadly speaking, into three categories: nobles who served; those who were subject to tax, and those, such as slaves, vagabonds and so on, who were not subject to tax because they had no independent legal status.

shall take suit against Dmitrii or his steward, then I, the Grand Princess, shall judge them, or my appointed boyar.

And whoever disobeys this my charter then let him be punished by me.

And the charter was granted in the year six thousand nine hundred and four, on January the fifteenth.

29

The restriction this will makes on the disposal by beneficiaries of their share of the land reflects the convention which gave family members the right to buy back land sold. It was as if landed property was regarded not as individual, but as family property [cp. 19]. Here a specific money value is attached to each lot.

The latter part of the document is concerned with the disposal of the villeins. 'Fully enslaved people' were those held by full deeds of bondage [see 33, 34]. These servile dependants (*kholopy*) came to be distinguished as 'full' slaves as many who were nominally bond slaves or villeins were in fact scarcely to be distinguished in status from dependent peasants (see p. 19). Moreover, at a higher functional level the villeins included a range of minor estate officials (servants, stewards, village overseers). The old meaning of the term *kholop* was lost and had to be replaced. A contributing factor, too, was the freeing of villeins. From the late fourteenth century the wills of the Grand Princes refer to the manumission of villeins and slaves on their death, but this seems likely to have amounted to a device for introducing greater flexibility into the organisation of the labour force. Certainly many of those nominally freed on the Prince's death will have continued in the same status with his successor.

We see from this document that such 'people' fled from their owners; and they were no doubt eagerly taken up by other landowners seeking hands.

The original of this will has not survived; the copy given here was made in 1641.

In the name of the Father and of the Son and of the Holy Ghost, I, the slave of God, the monk Iov, son of Prokofii, write my will being sound of mind, [indicating] what shall be given to whom, and what I am to take from whom.

I am to give Agrafena Borisova, wife of Semenovich, a poltina.[1]

As to my lands the hamlet of Sofronovskaya and all that has been subject to that hamlet from of old, I have given that land to my sister Matrona and my children, my son Timofei and Yakov and Ivan; and my children are to divide that land equally between them. If any son of mine does not want the land he shall not sell it to anyone apart from his brother, nor exchange, nor give it, but he shall take two rubles for his lot for that land. And my children themselves know the limits of that land by the old boundaries.

As to my land in Radonezh, Kharitonovskaya hamlet and Lnyanikovskaya waste and whatever has been subject to those lands from of old, with forest and meadows, those lands I have given to my son Andrei. And he knows the limits of those lands by the old boundaries. And if my son Andrei does not want the land he is not to sell it to anyone apart from his brothers, nor to exchange it, and he is to take six rubles from his brothers for that land.

I have given my fully enslaved people, male and female [as follows]; Nikiforets son of Mikhailov and the girl Marfitsa daughter of Roslyakov and the girl Marfitsa, too, daughter of Ivanik to my sister Matrona. I have given the boy Akulets, son of Mikiforik, and the woman Annitsa, daughter of Ivanik, to my son Timofei. I have given the woman Matrenitsa, daughter

----

[1] = half a ruble.

of Ivonka, with her daughter Arinitsya and the girl Afin'itsa, daughter of Roslyakov, to my son Andrei; I have given Loginets, son of Mikifor, and the woman Vasilisitsa, daughter of Ivonka, with her daughter Fedos'itsya, and Nikititsa, son of Siderik, to my son Yakov. I have given Simanets, son of Mikiforik, with his wife Ustin'itsa and their children Akulinitsya and Dar'itsya, to my son Ivan. I have given the girl Kilikeitsa, daughter of Login, to my granddaughter Nastasya, Andrei's daughter. As to my people who have fled from me, Sidorets, son of Semenka, Yarofeets, son of Ivanik, Griditsa, son of Bulat, Griditsa, son of Vasyuk, I have given those people to my children, to seek for themselves.

And I have ordered forty memorial services for my soul, a poltina to the great Nikola at Vskhodnikovo, a poltina to the Immaculate Virgin at Yakot', a poltina to the great Nikola at Ozertskoe.

And I have ordered to be set at liberty on my death my fully enslaved people: the woman Parashitsa, daughter of Ivonka, and the lad Panteleits, son of Yakush, and the woman Aksin'itsa, daughter of Sevast'yan, and the girl Akulinitsa, daughter of Sidorka.

As to my livestock, horses and horned and small cattle, rye grain in the earth and grain in the barn, that I have given to my sister Matrona and to my children.

And I have entrusted my sister[1] and children to my lord Mikhail Semenovich and Savost'yan Semenovich.

And at the [writing of the] will sat my spiritual father, Semion, abbot of [St] Nikola's, and Oleksandr Grigor'ev Semichov, Stepan Yakovlev Nelidov and the monk Elinarkh.

And the monk Ondreyan Shelepin wrote the will.

And we have all sealed this will with the one seal of Semen, abbot of [St] Nikola's.

On the reverse of the will is written: This will was shown to the Metropolitan of All Rus'; and the spiritual father,

---

[1] This refers to the woman who was his wife until he was shorn as a monk.

Semion, abbot of [St] Nikola's, and all the witnesses who are recorded in this will stood before Filip, Metropolitan of All Rus', and told the Metropolitan that his will was written in their presence; and the monk Ondrei Shelepin told the Metropolitan that he wrote this will. And according to the word of his lord the Metropolitan, the Metropolitan's clerk, Luka signed [this], the 18th of February in the year 78.

30

This deed, similar to [25–7], illustrates the continuing spread of limitations on peasant movement. 'People' and silver-men [see 25] are only to be withdrawn from the monastery by the Prince's officials at St George's day and on paying the money due.

6 December 1471. Charter of privilege by Prince Andrei Vasilevich Men'shii of Vologda to Abbot Ignatii of the St Cyril Monastery of Beloozero on the withdrawal of monastic peasants and silver-men at one date in the year — St George's day   ASEI, II, no. 193

For the sake of the Immaculate Virgin and her fair Assumption, in accordance with the deed of my father, the Grand Prince Vasilii Vasilevich, and the deed of my mother, the Grand Princess Mariya, now I, Prince Andrei Vasilevich, have granted a privilege to the Abbot Ignatii and the brethren of St Cyril's monastery, or whatever other abbot there shall be after him in that monastery, since they say their monastery people and silvermen are withdrawn from them before St George's day. And my representatives and volost heads and village overseers and free settlement officers and every sort of people, whoever they may be, are to withdraw all those their monastery people and silver-men from them [only] at the autumn St George's day, and after St George's day they are not to withdraw them. But when they withdraw, then they also pay the silver.

And the deed was granted at Vologda in the year 6980, December 6th, indict 5.

3 1

Here we have another example of a grant restricting peasant movement from a monastic estate. The prince's officials are to allow silvermen [see 25] to withdraw from the estate only at St George's day.

1462–81. Charter of privilege by Prince Andrei Vasilevich Men'shii of Vologda to the St Cyril of Beloozero monastery on the non-withdrawal of silver-men from monastery hamlets in Vologda, in Maslena, at any other date than St George's day
ASEI, II, no. 177

Now I, Prince Andrei Vasilevich, have granted a privilege to the monks of St Cyril's as to their hamlets on my estate in Vologda, in Maslena; they say they withdraw from them, from those hamlets, their people, St George's day silver-men, before the year, and I have granted [the request] of those monks: my princes and boyars and junior boyars and my village overseers, in accordance with this my charter, are not to withdraw the St George's day silver-men from those monks and from those monastery hamlets after St George's day. But if any one shall withdraw before St George's day or after St George's day, then that withdrawal is not [to be taken as] a withdrawal.

32

Ivan III laid down in this document the conditions on which monastery 'people' might be withdrawn from a monastery at Beloozero. If the money due to the monastery was agreed, it was to be paid; but if not, a guarantor acceptable to the monastery was to be found and the Grand Prince would later sit in judgement on the case [cp. 25]. The charter of privilege mentioned is the White Lake (Beloozero) Charter translated by Dewey (see p. 1).

In this document there is no mention of St George's day. This may mean that here there was no restriction as to the period when peasants could withdraw, or, more probably, that the restriction to movement at St George's day was sufficiently established for it to require no special mention.

April 1488–90. Deed and reading by the Grand Prince Ivan Vasilevich to Beloozero, to the town hundred-man, the reeves and peasants, in the little town of Fedos'in, to Vognema, Volochek Slovenskii, Irdma, Ugla, Cherepoves', Kistnema on the reckoning of 'silver' when peasants of the St Cyril Monastery, Beloozero, withdraw

ASEI, II, no. 276

From the Grand Prince Ivan Vasilevich of All Rus' to Beloozero to the town hundred-man and all the peasants, and to the little town of Fedos'in, and to Vognema, and to Volochek Slovenskii, to Ir'dma, and to Ugla and to Cherepoves' and to Kist'nema, to the reeves. Here the monks of the Immaculate Monastery of St Cyril, Gavrilo and Galasei, have petitioned me and say that you are withdrawing their monastery people, silver-men, from the main establishment and from the hamlets. And if any peasant is said to be guilty on their silver,[1] you should pay the monastery's silver, and carry their peasant away.

And if anyone is said not to be guilty to the monastery for silver, in that case you should give the monastery a surety, as they require, on their silver, [someone] whom they know, and those you should place before me, before the Grand Prince, at the same date as that which you have and is written in my, the Grand Prince's, charter of privilege, the Great Eve.[2] And having read this my deed, give it back to them.

The Grand Prince Ivan Vasilevich of All Rus'.

33

No deeds of full slavery [see 29] appear to have survived as independent documents. This is an extract from the note-book of Dmitrii Alyab'ev, a Novgorod clerk, in 1597; the document, however, refers to four generations and so probably originated late in the fifteenth century.

Late fifteenth century. Note of a deed of full [bondage] of Nastasiya Onanya and her daughter   ASEI, III, no. 406

The same day Fedor Redrov submitted an inventory and appended to the note of the report a deed of full [bondage] with a lead seal. And in the deed of full [bondage] it is written:

Nastas'ya wife of Onanya and her daughter Tat'yanitsa sold herself of her own will without [reference to] the usher, to Vasilii Borisovich's clerk, Ostanko, and his wife and his children finally as a full bond slave.[3] And they have taken two Novgorod rubles in Novgorod money.

---

[1] I.e. owing them money, either rents or loans.
[2] The eve of the week before Lent.
[3] *oderen' v polnitsu*; as if to say 'turfed into full bondage'. The custom of

And the witnesses have signed.

And according to that deed of full [bondage] of his grandfather, Vasilii, Boris's son, Istomko Ostap's son and his son Grishka; and his son Grishka in his household married Polageitsa and he had a son Mishka born as a slave. And that deed of full [bondage] when it was written was handed to Fedor Redrov.

34

Here we have it explicitly stated that the bond slaves mentioned are merely changing masters, selling themselves 'from full bondage to full bondage'. The deed makes it clear, however, that it was in reality essentially a transaction between the old and the new owner. As in [33], the family remain bound for many generations, in this case five. The only way out appears to be to run away.

Late fifteenth century. Note of a report deed relating to Andronik, his wife and children

RIB, XVII, no. 516, pp. 192–3

Deed of full [bondage]. Report of Vasilii Fedorovich; Mikhailo Tirkov bought from Esip Esipov, son of Ovtsyn, Andronik and his wife Matrenka and children, Stepanko, Portaseiko, Mauritsa, Nastas'itsa, Katerinetsa, from one full bondage to another, and gave eight rubles for them. And Andronik said that he, his wife and children sold themselves from full bondage to full bondage. The deed of full [bondage] has a wax seal impressed.

And in accordance with that full deed [of bondage] of their

placing a turf on the head to symbolise the importance of some act continued at least into the late nineteenth century (e.g. V. Antipov, in *Zhivaya starina*, vyp. I, god XV (1906), otdel I, 131.

great-great-grandfather, Mikhailo, [the following relatives] of that Ondronik and his children served them, but have now run away: Lavrenteiko, nicknamed Pervushka, son of Marko, and his brother Matyushka, Kiriko, Ivashko, and their sister Paraskov'itsa, the Olekseev children; and Kirilko and Ivashko live in Koper'e uezd, and their sister Paraskov'itsa is a runaway. And Mar'itsa, daughter of Orisim, nicknamed Belka, is a runaway.

35

We have seen several examples of ways in which peasant movement was being restricted in the fifteenth century. These have included grants made by the princes to landowners, frequently monasteries, and there have been variations in the terms of these grants and of the instructions issued to royal officials. Attempts to regulate the relationship between peasant and lord were somewhat haphazard and proceeded in piecemeal fashion. By the end of the fifteenth century, however, the predominance of Moscow was assured; the Tatars had been defeated, the authority of the Moscow Princes had been extended over a very considerable area and there was now no major challenge to Moscow's dominance. The Law Code of 1497 was at once both one of the results of these successes and also a further step towards strengthening the emergent Russian state.

The Law Code laid down regulations intended to apply to the whole area of the state and in this sense differed fundamentally from the individual grants with which we have so far been largely concerned. In part, as in articles 17–20 and 23, it was concerned with the administration of justice and the fees involved. These articles tried to ensure that documents relating to slaves were valid; only those who held a state appointment with rights of a boyar court could authorise charters of manumission; those without such rights (see article 20) had to appeal to boyars in Moscow in order to have the documents validated.

Article 56 established that villeins who escaped from Tatar captivity were thereby free. Such people could find themselves a place in the growing towns at this period and, incidentally, would there-fore become liable to taxation, thus contributing to the maintenance of the state.

The main article of the Law Code for us is article 57. In it the restriction of peasant movement to one period in the year, early in the winter, was laid down as a rule applying to all peasants. A clear-ance payment, to be paid on quitting a holding and called the dwelling payment, was also laid down; this was graded for the first four years of residence and a distinction was made between tene-ments in open land ('the fields') and those in the forest which had to pay only half the amount to which the former were liable. The reason for this was made clear in the 1550 Law Code [see 40]. The peasant, however, still had the right to move.

Extracts from the Law Code of 1497   PRP, III, 348-9, 355

17. On the title deed to a villein. For his seal the boyar is to have nine dengas a head for the villein and for the female slave from a title deed and from the charter of manumission, and the clerk an altyn[1] a head from the signature, and the junior clerk who writes a title deed or charter of manumission three dengas a head.

18. On the charter of manumission. But if anyone submits a charter of manumission without a boyar's appeal, and without the clerk's signature, or, in towns, without the royal represen-tative's appeal, that boyar [or representative] having a living with [the rights of] a boyar court, then that charter of manu-mission is not to be taken as a charter of manumission apart from that charter of manumission which a master writes in his own hand; and that charter of manumission is to be taken as a charter of manumission.

19. On an invalid court. If a boyar finds anyone guilty not in accordance with the court and grants a title deed against

---

[1] = 6 dengas.

him with the clerk, then that deed is not to be taken as a deed; and what has been taken is to be given back, but the boyar and the clerk are not liable to a fine for this, but the plaintiff is to be given justice anew.

20. On the royal representative's decree. But representatives and volost heads who hold livings without [the rights of] a boyar court are not to hand over a villein or a female slave without an appeal [to a boyar court], nor to issue deeds [against] runaways; nor without an appeal to issue title deeds to a villein or a female slave against their master, nor to issue charters of manumission to a villein or a female slave...

23. But for a villein and a female slave the seal-holder is to have nine dengas a head for a title deed, and the clerk is to have for the signature an altyn a head, and the junior clerk who writes the deed is to have three dengas a head...

56. But if the Tatar forces capture a villein and he flees from captivity, then he is free and not a villein to his old master.

57. On peasant withdrawal. And peasants are to withdraw from the volost, from village to village at one term a year, the week before St George's day in the autumn and the week after St George's day in the autumn. For their tenements [peasants are to] pay the dwelling payments [at the rate of] a ruble per tenement in the fields and a poltina[1] in the forests. But if any peasant lives under someone a year and goes off, he pays for a quarter of a tenement; but if he lives two years and goes off, he pays for half a tenement; but if he lives three years and goes off, he pays for three-quarters of a tenement; but if he lives four years, he pays for a whole tenement.

[1] = half a ruble.

36

This deed reflects part of the process of increasing state control. The grant of a living to the prince appointed to administer a volost over-rides any formerly issued grants of immunity. Grants of immunity frequently envisaged the terms of one grant being replaced by another [see 18]. The document also depicts the fairly detailed administrative organisation which existed in certain areas and gives some idea of the extent to which control over the countryside was already being exercised through various officers of justice.

The extant copy of this document is dated to the end of the seventeenth century.

29 June 1506. List of income given by Grand Prince Vasilii Ivanovich to the volost head Prince Yuri L'vovich Kozlovskii to a living[1] in Antonov stan. ASEI, III, no. 189

I, the Grand Prince Vasilii Ivanovich of All Russia, have granted Prince Yuri, son of Lev, Kozlovskii, that he have my grant, the volost of Antonov stan, and if anyone in that volost has my charters of privilege that they are not to give food dues to my governors, yet I, the Grand Prince, have [nevertheless] granted Prince Yuri and have ordered him to have his food dues in that volost from all boyar and monastic deed-holders according to this deed. And food dues per sokha[2] for the volost governor at Christmas: a side of meat, ten loaves, a mekh[3] of oats, a load of hay: and at Easter food dues per sokha for the volost governor: a side of meat, ten loaves; and on St Peter's

---

[1] A living (*kormlenie*) was a grant of dues, usually in kind and in services, made to officials appointed for the purpose of local administration.

[2] The term for the implement of cultivation was also used as a tax unit.

[3] A mekh was equivalent to a measure (*korobya*), details of which are given under [6] p. 37 n. 1.

day[1] per sokha a sheep, ten loaves. And if the volost governor does not desire the food dues he shall take ten dengas for a side of meat, ten dengas for ten loaves, eight dengas for a mekh of oats, ten dengas for a sheep, two altyns for a load of hay. And his servant shall have per sokha on all those three festivals half the food dues to the volost governor. And his court investigator shall have a due per sokha: at Christmas a loaf and a portion of meat, a zobnya[2] of oats; and at Easter per sokha the court investigator shall have a due of a loaf and a portion of meat, and on St Peter's day per sokha the court investigator shall have a due of a loaf and cheese. And if the justice shall not desire the due, he will take a denga for the loaf, a denga for the portion of meat, a denga for the cheese and two dengas for the zobnya of oats. And I have ordered for him to have food dues from six black[3] hamlets at Christmas, two altyns for a side of meat, two altyns for ten loaves, two altyns and a denga for a mekh of oats, two and a half altyns for a load of hay; and at Easter from six hamlets the food due to the volost governor shall be two altyns two dengas for a side of meat, two altyns for ten loaves; and at St Peter's day from six hamlets the food due to the volost governor shall be two altyns, two dengas for a sheep and two altyns for ten loaves. And his servant half that. And his court investigator's due from the hamlets at Christmas is three dengas, and at Easter his court investigator's due is two dengas and at St Peter's day his court investigator's due is again two dengas. And his court bailiff shall have a due from the hamlets, at Christmas eight dengas, and at Easter his court bailiff shall have a due from these hamlets four dengas and at St Peter's day his court bailiff shall have a due from these hamlets four dengas again.

[1] 29 June.

[2] The zobnya was equal to $\frac{1}{4}$ mekh (see p. 83 n. 3). In the commentary in PRP, III, 184, the zobnya, probably a Novgorod unit, is mistakenly equated with the Pskov zobnitsa, a unit of 2 mekhs.

[3] I.e. peasant, not belonging to monasteries or private landlords, but considered as subject to the Grand Prince.

I have also granted a privilege to Prince Yuri and ordered him to have the branding due in Antonov; if anyone buys a horse in that volost, or sells or exchanges one, they make a declaration before Prince Yuri or his brander and he shall brand their horses; and they take for the brand per horse a Moscow denga from the buyer and another Moscow denga from the seller; the names of the people and the horse's coat shall be written in a book for a record. If anyone in that volost buys a horse or sells or exchanges one and does not make a declaration before Prince Yuri or his brander beforehand and he discovers that, he shall take a fine and brand penalty from him, two Moscow rubles.

Written in Moscow in the year 7014, the 29th day of June.

On the reverse of the original deed is written: Grand Prince of All Russia.

A hanging seal of red wax with a two-headed eagle is on the original deed.

37

This is the earliest extant obligation to serve as a result of enserfment through debt; the copy dates from the end of the seventeenth century. As laid down in the 1497 Law Code [see 34] such a document had to be certified by a boyar court. The annual interest, evidently 20%, is not paid in money in this case, but worked off if the capital is repaid. If it is not repaid, Oksin'ya remains as a debt-slave; she is forbidden to escape from her obligation by appealing for the right to make annual payments of capital only on the basis of a terminable privilege [see 39] or by making some other contract not in writing.

1510. Obligation[1] to serve from a report about a loan to Oksin'ya wife of Mikhail D'yakonov,[2] son of Boris, from the report to the Ryazan' boyar Fedor Ivanovich Sunbul, the loan being of three rubles for a year from Iv. son of Oltuf'ya Koncheev, with the undertaking to work as interest

ASEI, III, no. 371

Copy for the Grand Princess Ogrofena from the report.

Report to the boyar of the Grand Princess Ogrofena, Fedor Ivanovich Sunbul; now I, Oksin'ya, wife of Mikhail D'yakon, have taken, master, from Ivan Duvan, son of Oltuf'ya Konchei, three rubles of money from the birth of John the Baptist for a year and I have given that money to my husband, Mikhail D'yakon, son of Boris. And for interest I am to go to work for Ivan Duvan; but if I do not want to work for him for the full term, I am to give him all his money together with the interest calculated, as they give six for five. But if the money is not paid on term, I am to work for him in the same way as interest, and I am not to take away from this deed of obligation by either [obtaining] a terminable privilege or a verbal obligation.

And at the appeal were Pa[n]krat, son of Mikhail Katov, and Semen, son of Timofei Denizhnikov, in the year 7018.

And the clerk of the Grand Princess, Fedor Matveev, signed it.

The original has a seal of black wax.

[1] An obligation (*kabala*) was a contract, usually relating to a debt, in which one side had the whip hand.
[2] It is possible that the man was 'Michael the deacon'.

38

We have had several references to inquisitions and the registration of peasants on estates [10, 24, 28, etc.]. It seems probable that only gradually in the course of the late fifteenth century did the wholesale inquisitions characteristic of sixteenth and seventeenth century Russia emerge. The contents of the registers, in some respects resembling cadastral surveys, resulting from the inquisitions varied with time and place. Here we have an extract describing a service estate in a western area, between Pskov and Smolensk, towards the middle of the sixteenth century.

In this document 'people' are differentiated from 'peasants' [see also 50]. The former are evidently villeins or in-servants at or by the home of the four younger brothers; the peasants live on their own holdings but are liable to a range of obligations in both money, kind and labour. There are also tenements without arable, the holders presumably making their living from a craft or trade in many cases, and labourers who worked for others. 'Arrivals' are also mentioned.

Throughout the translation of this extract 't.' stands for 'tenement'.

1540. Extract from the register of Toropets

Arkheograficheskii ezhegodnik za 1963 god, 349–50

Also in Dubna the service estate held by Stepan, Grigorii, Fedor, Burnash, and Kirei, sons of Vasilii Porokhov. Bobrovo hamlet: in a t. Stepan Porokhov himself; arable land in a field 12 chets; hay 50 stacks.[1] Obrubovo hamlet: in a t. Demeshko

---

[1] The phrase 'in a field' indicates that the stated area of land was a third of the total area, dispersed in the settlement's conventional three fields; it was assumed in such registers that the three courses in the settlement's open fields were of equal area. A chet (or *chetvert'*, literally 'a quarter') was half a desyatina, or probably nearly one and a half acres at that time. A stack (*kopna*)

Mikulin; in a t. Oleshko Ofonasov; in a t. Grichikha Lystsov; arable land in a field 20 chets, hay 45 stacks; in a t. the labourer Sen'ka Fomin without arable.

On the river Dvina. Zabolot'e Velikoe hamlet: in a t. Grigorii himself and Fedor, Burnash and Kirei Porokhov; and their people: in a t. Ofonasko; in a t. Starko; and their peasants: in a t. Ovdeiko Semenov and his brother Fed'ko; in a t. Fomka Shvarev; in a t. Ivashko Zubov; in a t. Vashura Fed'kov; in a t. Kuzemka Trufanov; in a t. Kur'yanko Titov; in a t. Ivashko Mikhnov; in a t. Fed'ka Pantyukhov; in a t. Frol Mikhnov; in a t. Pantyukh Mikhnov; in a t. Onosko Torasov; arable land in a field 100 chets, hay 270 stacks and a t. without arable of Ivashko Tarasov, and to that same hamlet, the hamlet of Sava Mityukov Palka has been let into the field. Strug hamlet: in a t. Ermolka Volin; in a t. Vas'ka Gurnev; in a t. Stepan's fellow Sheiko; arable land in a field 14 chets, hay 40 stacks. Ermolkovo hamlet: in a t. Mikulka Ivanov; in a t. Rosol Sidorov; in a t. Ignatko Mikhalev; arable in a field 10 chets, hay 15 stacks, and 2 tenements without arable of Klimyatka and Ivashko. Danilov hamlet above the Podnikla stream: in a t. Ortemko Mikulin; in a t. Vas'ko Ivanov; in a t. the labourer Yupa; arable in a field 10 chets, hay 25 stacks. Glinkovo hamlet: in a t. Olferko Rodin; in a t. Maksimko Shvar[ev]; in a t. Ontyushko Khvorov; arable land in a field 20 chets, hay 30 stacks. Chernevo hamlet: in a t. Klimyatka Ostaf'ev; in a t. Shiryai Ivanov; in a t. Ivanko Mikhalev; arable land in a field 10 chets, hay 25 stacks. Pirogovo hamlet: in a t. Kur'yanko Brazhlov; in a t. Rodya the arrival; in a t. Mishko the arrival; in a t. also Mishko the arrival; in a t. Nogovitsa; arable land in a field 20 chets, hay 25 stacks. Skoryanovo hamlet: in a t. Moseiko Pashutin; in a t. Ivashko Kharin; arable land in a field 11 chets, hay 22 stacks. Zaluzh'e hamlet: in a t. Ortemko Mikulin; in a t. Savkov Ivanov; arable land in a field 9 chets, hay 10 stacks. Zhabera hamlet on the

of hay was roughly a cone in shape; in the seventeenth century it seems to have been 16 feet up and over and 21 feet in circumference.

Zhabera stream: in a t. Ortemko Klimov; in a t. Dmitr Buya-nov; in a t. Savka Zakhar'in; arable land in a field 9 chets, hay 25 stacks. Zhabera hamlet also: in a t. Onfimko Ignatov; in a t. Kuritsa Onisimov; arable land in a field 10 chets, hay 15 stacks.

And the total held by Stepan and his brothers is 14 hamlets, and the tenements in them, apart from the two landlord's tenements, are 46; and the people in them, 3 of theirs, and peasants in them 47, and 3 tenements without arable land; arable land in one field 255 chets, hay 597 stacks.

And Stepan and his brothers take income from that service estate, 2 rubles 17 altyns and 2 moskovkas in money; and the grain income is 54 [chets] of rye, 108 chets of oats, 27 chets of barley malt, 13½ chets of wheat, 7 chets of peas and hemp, 13½ chets of hops, 18 bundles of flax; and the petty income is 18 sheep, 18 sides of meat, 36 hens, 18 hares, 18 grouse, 18 cheeses, 18 sheepskins, 18 shearlings, 1½ puds and 12 grivenkas of butter, 6 puds of honey, 18 loads of hay.[1]

And an item of income for them is the fishery in Lake Okhvat; the fish in it are every sort of white fish.[2]

And the vyts[3] they hold are 20 vyts in their old service estate; and the arable land in sokha units amounts to half a sokha, and they have all been granted additionally 26 vyts.

And their forest between the hamlets in all fields comes to 800 desyatinas.

And the peasants cultivate for them 2 fields[4] Ploska and Fofanovich; the arable land on them is 6 chets.

---

[1] The income appears to be calculated in conventional rather than real terms. The grain income is in units of 108 and those obtained by dividing by 2 (54, 27, 13½ and 7 (presumably a rounding of 6¾)); these do not appear to be conveniently related to numbers of peasants, tenements or size of area. Similarly, the petty income is mostly in units of 36, 18, or 6.

[2] White fish are elsewhere in this register listed as bream, pike, roach, perch and asp.

[3] A vyt' was literally a 'share', 'portion'. As a tax unit in such service areas it seems to have measured from 12 to 16 chetverts depending on the quality of the land.

[4] I.e. isolated fields (*nivy*), not fields in the sense of courses in a rotational system.

39

Here we have an example of the terminable privileges which authorised annual payment of the capital sum of a debt and excused the debtor further interest and the necessity to provide guarantees. Such privileges provided a possible way of escaping from over-burdensome obligations, so those drawing up such deeds sometimes included a clause intended to prevent any appeal for such a privilege [see 37].

26 January 1546. Terminable privilege of the Grand Prince Ivan Vasil'evich allowing the widow Palageya Glebovna Klishkova and her children to pay her debt to her creditors in the course of five years and without interest

Akty Yushkova, no. 149

Copy from a deed.

Now I, the Grand Prince, Ivan Vasil'evich of All Russia have granted a privilege in Kostroma uezd, Edoma volost, to Palageya, Gleb's daughter, wife of Karp Klishkov, from Mstislavl', and her children, Stepanko and Mitka and Ivashka, as she petitioned me and said that her husband Karp was in my service this spring and arrived back from his service ill and now he is no longer among the living; and afterwards his wife and children were left in debt and of his own accord he had written his wife and children and incidental people into those deeds of obligation; and in that they were endebted by those deeds of obligation and without such deeds, and by transfer notes and by notes of guarantee; and those creditors are suing them for that debt, but they have nothing with which to pay that debt. And I would grant them favour as regards that debt and give them my terminable privilege, let them pay that debt to their creditors as regards capital, without interest. So let it be, as Palageya petitioned me and said; and I, the Grand Prince, have granted and given Palageya, Karp's wife, and her children Stepanko and Mitka and Ivashka, this my terminable privilege for five years for that debt; and in those five years they are to pay their creditors that debt as regards capital, without interest. And our Kostroma representative and volost heads and their servants, court bailiffs and court investigators as regards that debt do not make them, or their guarantors who are recorded in obligations and without obligations in notes, give guarantees, and they are not to exact that debt from them; and our Moscow week officials as regards that debt do not make them give guarantees either and do not impose a term on them until that term of years [indicated]. The deed given in Moscow, the 26th day of January, in the year 7054.

On the reverse is written: the Grand Prince Ivan Vasil'evich of All Rus'.

A hanging seal of red wax.

[On the reverse:] Aleksandr Dmitreev Klishkov took the original deed, and I, Aleksandr Klishkov, put my hand to this copy.

40

The Law Code of 1550, while still recognising the peasant right to move at the time of St George's day, is more explicit than the Law Code of 1497 see [35]. It attempted to define what qualified as the forest zone, for which there was a reduced dwelling payment, and the tenement liable to that payment was defined as what was within the gates, i.e. the farm and its buildings within the yard. Later, in the seventeenth century, lords attempted to 'transfer many households into a single household' in order to reduce the incidence of taxation, presumably making use of this definition of a household or tenement see [54]. In a broader sense the same term (*dvor*) continued, like our own tenement, to mean both farm buildings and the farm lands and common rights. The article shows that the lower rate of dwelling payment for tenements in the forest, already laid down in the 1497 Law Code, depended on there being adequate building timber available. Where building timber, and, presumably, other forest resources, were not available in open non-forest land, the payment was at the higher rate.

We have already seen that early in the fifteenth century a priest's son might live apart from his father and eat his own bread [10]. The parish clergy were in many ways indistinguishable from other peasants and the concession here granted them was probably an attempt to secure their support.

The latter part of article 88 lays down a new regulation: a peasant selling himself into bondage may leave at any time. It has been suggested that this was a concession Ivan IV's government felt obliged to make to the great nobles who still retained numbers of villeins, even though the government favoured the gentlemen who held service tenure; these probably had fewer such dependants.

Extract from the Law Code of 1550
PRP, IV, 258

88. But peasants are to withdraw from volost to volost, from village to village at one time a year, the week before St George's day in the autumn and the week after St George's day in the autumn. And for tenements [peasants are to] pay the dwelling payment, a ruble and two altyns for a tenement in the fields, but in the forests where there are ten verstas[1] of forest suitable for building a poltina and two altyns for a tenement. But any peasant who lives under someone for a year and goes off, he pays for a quarter of a tenement; if he lives for two years he pays for half a tenement; but if he lives for three years, he pays for three-quarters of a tenement; if he lives for four years, he pays for the whole tenement, a ruble and two altyns. And the dwelling payment is to be had from the gates. And the cartage

---

[1] A versta was approx. ⅔ mile, so this amounts to roughly 7 miles.

due is to be had from the tenement at the rate of two altyns; and apart from that he is liable to no customary dues. But if any peasant has grain remaining in the ground, when he reaps that grain, he shall give from that grain or standing crop a sheep [as boundary payment], two altyns; but if at any time his rye was in the land, he pays the Tsar's and the Grand Prince's due from the rye and he is not liable to the boyar's labour rent [with that lord] under whom he lived. And a priest is not liable to the dwelling payment and he can go off without term. But if any peasant sells himself from the arable as a full slave, he goes off without term and he is not liable to the dwelling payment; but if any of his grain remains in the ground, he pays from that grain the Tsar's and the Grand Prince's due; but if he does not want to pay the due, he is deprived of his grain in the ground.

41

In this deed of obligation [see also 33, 37] the peasant borrowing money from the monastery undertakes not merely to till the land, but also to build a house. If he fails to fulfil his obligation he is liable to twice the sum borrowed. It is evident, however, that the obligation was undertaken not by the peasant alone, but by his children also; the obligation lasted for more than one generation.

1552–3. 'Rural deed of obligation' of Moisei son of Nifant and his children with the Saviour Monastery of Priluka [i.e. the area near Luka] for one ruble on condition he lives in the monastery's hamlet of Levashevo PRP, IV, 70

Now I, Mosei son of Nifant, and my children, Istoma and Nikifor, have taken from Antonii, cellarer of the Saviour of

Priluka a ruble of the monastery's treasury money from St George's day in the autumn till St George's day for a year. And for that money we are to till a third [of the arable] of their hamlet,[1] Levashevo, and I am to build a house. But if I do not begin to live at Levashevo on a third, then we are liable to pay 2 rubles according to this obligation. And I am to pay the quit-rent according to the registers. And whichever of us is present, he is liable to the tillage or the money.

And the witnesses to this: Elizarii Yakov's son from Levashevo and Oleksei Kiril's son.

And the monastery clerk Volod'ka Yakim's son wrote the deed, the year 7060 first.

[After the text:] Died.

[On the reverse:] Four grivnas paid on this obligation. Levashevo. For a child,[2] and he lives at Tot'ma.

42

This instruction, issued as the result of an appeal to the Tsar from elected peasant officials, presumably of a commune, gives us some insight into how the regulations laid down in the Law Codes and other enactments were applied in practice. On great estates landholders harass peasants who wish to move to the crown estates; they obstruct the legal work of the peasant elected heads who act as withdrawal officials recruiting labour for the black lands; they overcharge peasants if they do leave. The Tsar instructs his officers in Novgorod to send an official to help the peasants and ensure that they pay only the amounts laid down.

[1] The lands of the hamlet were divided between different owners and Moisei was to till a third of the total cultivated area.
[2] A 'child' (ditenysh or detenysh) was a monastery's 'servant' (sluga), i.e., a peasant who had sometimes grown up on the monastery's land and worked it in return for pay or food.

5 September 1555. Instruction of Ivan IV to the Novgorod clerks Fedor Syrkov and Kazarin Dubrovskii on assistance to the elected heads of the Pustorzheva black[1] hamlets in removing peasants from the junior boyars at the indicated terms

PRP, IV, III

From the Tsar and Grand Prince Ivan Vasil'evich of All Russia to our estate, Great Novgorod, to our clerks Fedor Syrkov and Kazarin Dubrovskii. The elected heads of the black stans, Chyuneiko Levont'ev, Manko Vasil'ev, Protasko Fedorov, Borisko Yakovlev and Ofonasko Knyazev, in place of all the peasants of both halves of Rzheva Pustaya, have petitioned me from Rzheva Pustaya. They say that the Rzheva, Pskov, Luka junior boyars and those of other jurisdictions remove our peasants from the Rzheva black hamlets to live with them as their peasants not in accordance with the term, but at all times and without the customary dues, and, they say, withdrawal officials come to them from our Rzheva hamlets with withdrawals, on term, of peasants due to withdraw to them to our black Rzheva hamlets and if any peasants want to go to live in those our black hamlets, those junior boyars, they say, beat those withdrawal officials, and put them in irons and do not let the peasants go from them, but seizing them, torment and plunder them, put them in irons and, allegedly, take from them a dwelling payment not as laid down in the Law Code, but five or ten rubles; and, they say, it is impossible for them [i.e. the elected heads] to withdraw peasants from those junior boyars.

And if the elected heads Chyuneiko Levont'ev and his fellows start to petition you against any junior boyars and small freeholders, men of Rzheva, Pskov or Luka, [claiming] that they do not let their peasants go at term to live in our Rzheva black

---

[1] See [36], p. 84 n. 3.

95

hamlets on their withdrawal, you should grant them a junior clerk, or whomever suits, and should order him, with those elected heads, Chyuneiko Levont'ev and his fellows, to withdraw at term the peasants from those junior boyars and small freeholders to our black Rzheva hamlets. And you should order those peasants to pay the quittance payment in accordance with our decree.

Written in Moscow the 5th day of September, the year 7064.

43

This list of obligations from documents of the St Nicholas Monastery of Krasnyi Kholm, Antoniev stan, illustrates the extent to which monasteries acted as money-lenders and acquired work hands in the process. The dependants acquired in this way seem to have been able to get out of debt by no means in every case; many died in debt. It is impossible, however, to make a complete analysis from the details given in this document. Moreover, it should be remembered that this period in the late sixteenth century included the very disturbed time of internal dissension and the disruptive activities of Ivan IV's oprichnina.

Not earlier than 1581. Extract from a note of existing notes of obligation in a monastic treasury   MIK XVI v. p. 61

From the year 7030 even to the year 7071[1] [we have] 270 and one escheated notes of obligation. The borrowers in these cases died and in these [deeds] 269 rubles, 3 altyns, 4 dengas were promised to be taken in money. And on these same notes of obligation 44 chetverts[2] of grain, rye and oats were to be taken.

[1] I.e. 1521 to 1563.
[2] A chetvert was about 2 bushels, or roughly 1 cwt. of rye or $\frac{3}{4}$ cwt. of oats See Glossary for further details.

From the year 7006 even to the year 7052[1] [we have], of old obligations, the borrowers having died, and of deposits [i.e. mortgages], 211 obligations and 2 records of obligations; and in them 378 rubles 5 dengas were promised to be taken. And the total money on the obligations in the treasury both known and not known, old and new, is 831 rubles 23 altyns and a denga. And in the year 79[2] the treasury handed out obligations, and the money on them was 45 rubles 15 altyns. And of the money given back, oats was bought for 18 rubles for the monastery's use in the same year, and 27 rubles placed in the treasury. And the known obligations for life are 54; in them are 263 chetverts of rye, 350½ chetverts of oats, 21½ chetverts of barley and 2 chetverts of wheat.

From the year 7020 to the year 7075[3] the borrowers concerned in 150 old obligations died; in them the grain promised to be taken was 513 chetverts of rye and 683½ chetverts of oats, 2½ chetverts of wheat.

From the year 7019 to the year 7052[4] the borrowers concerned in 115 obligations died and dispersed; and in them the grain promised to be taken was 771½ chetverts of rye and a third, and 429 chetverts of oats, and 25 chetverts of barley, 20 chets of wheat. There are 15 old grain obligations and a memorandum; 38½ chetverts of rye and 15 chetverts of oats, and 5 chetverts of barley, 1½ chetverts of wheat. And the total of grain obligations, known and unknown, old and new, is 335 obligations; and the grain to be taken in them is 1586½ chetverts of rye, and 1485 chetverts of oats, 24 chetverts of wheat. And the total grain is 3171[5] chetverts. And as regards those obligations, old ones, money ones and grain ones, the borrowers have died and dispersed and there is no one from whom to take [the money or grain].

From the year 7081 to the year 7089[6] 72 money obligations

---

[1] 1497 to 1544.   [2] (15)70/1.
[3] 1511 to 1567.   [4] 1510 to 1544.
[5] Evidently an error; the totals for rye and oats amount to 3071½ chetverts.
[6] 1572 to 1581.

were added to the treasury compared with the old registers; and the money to be taken on them 130 rubles: on 40 obligations 80 rubles, and on 30 obligations there were 50 rubles of money. And as regards those 30 obligations the borrowers died out and dispersed; there is no one from whom to take. And 50 grain obligations less two were added to the treasury, and on [30] obligations 450½ chetverts of every sort of grain is to be taken and 209 chetverts of grain on 18 obligations. And as regards those 18 obligations there is no one from whom to take grain, the borrowers have died and dispersed from God's dispensation, from grain failure.

44

In November, 1597, this decree was issued giving landlords the right to reclaim peasants who had run away in the course of the preceding five years if they had submitted petitions for their return. In the early 1590s, and also, in all probability, from 1581, there had been various temporary remissions of the peasant right of departure which had been granted in the Law Codes of 1497 [see 35] and 1550 [see 40]. This, together with the disturbed times, led to increased numbers of peasants running away and to a flood of petitions for their return. Behind this there lay the struggle for work hands between the great nobles and other large land-holders who were capable of paying off peasant debts, on the one hand, and, on the other, lesser land-holders and servitors with fewer resources who were frequently absent on the Tsar's campaigns [see 39]. It seems probable that the five-year term was decided on because there had been a number of inquisitions carried out in 1592 and 1593 and the registers then drawn up could be used as a basis in any cases arising.

In this period the term 'people' is sometimes used, as in the first sentence of this document, to mean servitors. The increasingly regularised complexities of social ranks are reflected in the document both by the ranks being listed and also by the formal and repetitious language itself. This process, though, was to continue [see 45, 50, etc.].

24 November 1597. Decree on runaway peasants

PIK, no. 32 (reprinted from AI, I, no. 221, III)

The 24th day of November, 7106, the Tsar and Grand Prince Fedor Ivanovich of All Russia decreed and the boyars assented:

If any peasants of boyars or of gentlemen or of Department people or of junior boyars or of any people holding land by service or inheritance, or of the Patriarch's or metropolitans' or bishops' or monastic estates, have run away five years prior to the present year 106, then against those runaway peasants in their flight and against those service and heritable tenants on whose lands they live after running away, those service tenants from whom they have run away and the Patriarchal and metropolitan and episcopal junior boyars and the stewards and servants of monastic villages are to be given justice and to seek out firmly by any search and, in accordance with justice and the search, to take back those runaway peasants with their wives and children and all their livestock, wherever each one lived. And [as to] any peasants who ran away six or seven or ten or more years before the present year 106, those service and heritable tenants from whom they ran away and the Patriarchal and metropolitan and episcopal junior boyars and the stewards and servants of monastic estates against those runaway peasants of theirs in their flight, and against those service and heritable tenants on whose lands they live after running away six or seven or ten or more years prior to the present year 106, have not petitioned the Sovereign Tsar and Grand Prince Fedor Ivanovich of All Russia; and the Sovereign Tsar and Grand Prince Fedor Ivanovich of All Russia has decreed and in accordance with the decree of the Sovereign Tsar and Grand Prince Fedor Ivanovich of All Russia the boyars have assented: against those runaway peasants in their flight and against those service and heritable tenants on whose lands they live after running away they are not to be given justice and are not to take them back wherever each one lived.

And in accordance with the decree of the Sovereign Tsar and Grand Prince Fedor Ivanovich of All Russia and the assent of the boyars: any peasants of boyars and of gentlemen and of Department people and of junior boyars and of any people holding land by service or inheritance, and of the Patriarch's, metropolitan's, bishops' and of monastic estates who have run away five years prior to the present year, 106, against those peasants in their flight and against those service and heritable tenants on whose lands they live after running away, the service and heritable tenants from whom they ran away and the Patriarchal and metropolitan and episcopal junior boyars and the stewards and servants of monastic estates are to be given justice and to seek out firmly by any search; and in accordance with justice and the search they are ordered to take back those runaway peasants with their wives and children and all their livestock where each one lived. But if any peasants of service and heritable tenants and of the Patriarch's, metropolitan's, bishops' and monastic estates ran away six and seven and ten and more years prior to the present year 106, those service and heritable tenants and the Patriarchal and metropolitan and episcopal junior boyars and stewards and servants of monastic estates from whom they have run away have not petitioned the Sovereign Tsar and Grand Prince Fedor Ivanovich of All Russia against those runaway peasants of theirs in their flight and against those service and heritable tenants on whose lands they live when they have run away from them six and seven and ten and more years prior to the present year, 106, and they are to be refused and not to be granted justice against those runaway peasants and against those service and heritable tenants on whose lands they live after running away, but they are to be granted justice and search against runaway peasants who ran away five years prior to the present year, 106. But [as to] any cases against runaway peasants which are before the courts and have not been completed prior to the present decree of the Sovereign Tsar and Grand Prince Fedor Ivanovich of All Russia, the Sovereign Tsar and Grand Prince Fedor Ivanovich of All Russia has decreed and in accordance with the decree of the Sovereign Tsar and Grand Prince Fedor Ivanovich the boyars have assented: to complete [such] cases in accordance with justice and the search.

45

In 1601 there was famine in Russia and the situation was such that concessions had to be made to the peasants. They were given the right to move. The servitors also had to be placated because the Tsar, Boris Godunov, did not feel secure in his authority; he had been elected Tsar in 1598 after the last heir of the Rurik dynasty had died in mysterious circumstances. Unlike the crown, the church and the court, therefore, the servitors were permitted to move their peasants. At the same time, however, everyone was allowed to move one or two peasants, but not more. The confusion caused by this uncertain decision is referred to in [46]. The formal grounds for rescinding the decree on which this memorandum was based was that it had been issued by Tsar Boris without boyar assent.

The document gives a useful picture of the numerous categories serving the Tsar, his wife and his heir, both throughout the country, in the towns, in Moscow itself and attendant on the Tsar, and also in the Great Palace.

28 November 1601. Memorandum on peasant release to the chamberlain Morozov

PIK, no. 33 (reprinted from *AAE*, II, no. 20)

28th day of November, 7110, a memorandum to the chamberlain Vasilii Petrovich Morozov according to the decree of the

Sovereign Tsar and Grand Prince Boris Fedorovich of All Russia. In the present year 110 the Great Sovereign Tsar and Grand Prince Boris Fedorovich of All Russia and his son the Great Sovereign Tsarevich, Prince Fedor Borisovich of All Russia, have granted and have ordered the peasants in all their state to be given the right to move because of taxation and fines. And gentlemen who are selected to serve, and those attending the Sovereign Tsar and the Grand Prince Boris Fedorovich of All Russia and with the Sovereign Tsarevich, the Prince Fedor Borisovich of All Russia, and the town junior boyars and the town stewards of all towns and every foreigner and the in-servants of every rank of the Great Palace, butlers, bearers of insignia, cup-bearers, under-butlers, the stewards of the Stables Department and the stirrup grooms, and bearers of insignia and the huntsmen and mounted kennel men of the Hunt Section, the gerfalconers, falconers and hawkers of the Falconry Section the trumpeters and pipers, and the junior boyars of the Lady Tsaritsa and the Grand Princess Mariya Grigorevna of All Russia, and the junior clerks of all Departments, and the muske-teer hundred-men and cossack commanders of the Musketeer Department, and the translators and dragomen of the Am-bassadors' Department, and the patriarchal, metropolitan, arch-episcopal and episcopal Department people, junior boyars, between themselves, are to withdraw and move peasants. And the term for the peasants to withdraw and move is St George's day in the autumn and two weeks after St George's day. And the peasant is to pay as dwelling payment a ruble two altyns for his tenement. But in crown villages and in black volosts, and those of the Patriarch, the metropolitans, the archbishops, the bishops and monasteries and the boyars, chamberlains and the great gentlemen and the Department people and the clerks and sewers, the bearers of insignia and the musketeer com-manders, they are ordered not to move peasants in the present year, 110. And in Moscow uezd all people between themselves and from other towns in Moscow uezd are likewise not to withdraw and not to move peasants. But any people between themselves, in the present year 110, may move peasants and they, in accordance with the decree of the Sovereign Tsar and Grand Prince Boris Fedorovich of All Russia, are to move between themselves to one man from one other man one peasant or two, but no one is to move three or four to one from one [other].

46

This document refers to two others given above [44, 45] in its introductory section. Its main provision, however, is to establish the right of search for fifteen years. Such terms of years were counted from the date when the runaway had fled. Claims were to be based on the surveys carried out in 1592 and 1593 [see 44].

The specific mention of the fact that the dwelling payment was three rubles for a bachelor, the same as for a tenement, shows that the normal peasant unit was the farm run by a family, those who 'live together with their father and their mother, and not apart from them' [56, §28; cp. 56, §24 and 10, §12]. This conclusion is reinforced by the provisions aimed at facilitating early marriage, a behaviour pattern characteristic of eastern Europe (see J. Hajnal's remarks in D. V. Glass and D. E. C. Eversley (eds.), *Population in history* (1965), pp. 101–3).

9 March 1607. Statute of the assembly of Tsar Vasilii Shuiskii on peasants and villeins   *PRP*, IV, 586–9

On the 9th day of March, 7115, the Sovereign Tsar and Grand Prince Vasilii Ivanovich of All Russia with his father [confessor] the Most Holy Hermogen, the Patriarch, with all the Holy Chapter and with his Tsar's Synclitos, have heard the report of the Service-tenure House from the boyars and clerks that, as they allege, by the transfer of peasants there had been caused great disturbances, scandals and violence by the powerful against the weak, which, they say, there had not been under Tsar Ivan Vasilevich because peasants had [the right of] free departure; but Tsar Fedor Ivanovich in accordance with the admonition of Boris Godunov, not listening to the Council of the senior boyars, forbad departure for the peasants, and he drew up registers of whoever then had several peasants anywhere, and afterwards from that many enmities, disturbances and law suits began. Tsar Boris Fedorovich, seeing great disturbance in the people, abandoned those registers and granted [the right of] transfer to the peasants, yet not entirely, so that the judges did not know how to complete cases in accordance with this. And now in that matter great dissensions and violence have been caused and to many ruin and fatal murder and much brigandage and plunder on the roads has been and is taking place.

On account of this we have issued an edict and laid down in accordance with the holy oecumenical chapters and with the rules of the holy fathers [as follows].

Any peasants who for 15 years before this date were recorded in the registers of the year 101[1] are to be under those under whom they were registered; but if those peasants have departed to anyone else and in that matter there is a petition against those peasants, or against those who hold them, and those cases are not completed, or if anyone shall petition up to the 1st September this year,[2] those peasants are to be given up according to those registers with their wives and children and all their property to those under whom they were registered, up to Christmas of the year 116[3] without dwelling payment; and if anyone shall not give them up by that date, then he shall be charged for acceptance and the dwelling payment in accordance with this statute; and if there was no petition for any

[1] 1592/3.
[2] I.e. up to the new year, since the year then started with 1 September.
[3] 1607/8.

peasants to date, and shall be none by 1st September, then those shall not be given up [according to those registers after that date], but they shall be recorded in the registers to those under whom they now live and henceforth for fifteen years there shall be no cases relating to peasants and peasants shall not be exported [nor returned].

But if there be any who, henceforth, leaving one [lord], transfer to anyone else at all, and he to whom he comes accepts him contrary to this our statute of the Assembly, the peasant, having been seized from him, shall be transferred with all his goods whence he had fled; and for the tenement, if that peasant had built one, [the lord] shall pay what is judged, but he shall not take the tenement; and the Tsar shall demand from him [i.e. the landowner], because he accepted the peasant contrary to the statute, 10 rubles; do not accept another's [peasant]; and as dwelling payment from him [i.e. the accepting landowner] to him whose peasant it was, three rubles for each year for the tenement, and also three rubles a year for a bachelor.

And if a peasant shall come to anyone to hire himself for work for summer or for winter or for the whole year, but not in families, and whoever hires him [takes him] for not more than a year, he is not guilty for accepting him and no dwelling payment shall be exacted; because his lord knows where he lives.

But if a woman or widow or maid flees to someone else's estate and marries, that peasant who takes to wife another's woman shall be given to him to whom the woman belongs with all his property and the children born of that runaway; and if that man has children of his first wife, there is no case against them, they are not to be given back with the stepmother; but if they are small, then let them go with their father until one passes 15 years old.

But if any people hold a slave girl, a maid up to 18 years, or a young widow more than two years after her husband [has died], or an unmarried youth of 20 years or more, and do not marry them and do not grant them freedom, then that widow or maid or youth is to go to the Treasurer; and the Treasurer after enquiring about it and concluding that they have passed those years and the lord does not marry them, then in Moscow the Treasurer is to give them charters of manumission and the royal representatives and justices in other towns; but if their lord petitions against them in regard to theft or goods carried off, then they [those officials] shall refuse him in this and not give justice; do not hold the unmarried contrary to the law of God and the rules of the holy fathers, and fornication and filthy activities shall not multiply among the people.

And if after this statute any peasant or villein or a female slave shall run away from a lord and come to another, the lord is to seek his villein and female slave and peasant in fifteen years [from their flight], but beyond fifteen years he is not to seek and is not to be given justice.

And in the towns the royal representatives, military commanders and justices and clerks and every sort of Department people are to enquire throughout their uezd or competence through the reeves and the hundred-men and the clergy whether there are not new arrivals anywhere, and when they tell him [that there are any], he is to take them and firmly question them; whose he is, where from, when he ran away and where and for how long he lived and whether anyone did not incite him; and if he says someone incited him and produces evidence against him, this instigator is to be punished with the market-place punishment[1] and a guarantee is to be taken from him so that he takes back that runaway to his lord; and a fine of 10 rubles is to be taken from him to the treasury; and from every one of those who accepted him [i.e. the runaway] and kept him more than 7 days in the village there are to be exacted 10 rubles to the treasury per tenement and per man on his own, and 3 rubles for accepting a woman and for a maid.

But if they accept someone's villein or peasant or woman in villages or volosts of the Tsar and Grand Prince or in black

---

[1] I.e. beaten with the knout in the market-place. See [56], article 27.

volosts or in Patriarchal and prelatic and monastic villages, then for accepting [them] exaction is to be made from the volost heads [or the stewards] and the reeve who was then administering that volost and accepted the arrival; and dwelling payments for the tenements are to be had from those villages and volosts, and in towns, from all artisan quarter people in accordance with this statute.

But if any royal representative or justice or clerk and other Department person shall not enquire about, search out and question about arrivals in his uezd[1] and does not take the money for accepting them, and they report him in this, the money is to be exacted from him twofold and he is to be thrown out from the matter and henceforward he is to have no part in any affair of the Sovereign.

47

This 'concession' is an illustration of one way in which deals in peasants developed. By this means peasants could be transferred from one lord to another; at the same time this was a convenient way for the smaller-scale landlords to cut their losses when their peasants fled to those more powerful than themselves.

1619/20. Note of a concession of two peasants of Vladimir uezd by the service tenant, Dorofei, son of Vasilii Pisarev, to the Trinity Monastery of St Sergius   PRP, v, 61–2

Now I, Dorofei Vasil'ev Pisarev, of Kashira in the present year 128 have petitioned the great lord, the most holy Filaret, Patriarch of Moscow and All Russia, about my runaway peasants, Trenka Ivanov, son of Tur, and Ivashka Bogdanov,

[1] *v ego v ezde* (on his journey) is probably a corruption.

that those peasants, running away from me, lived in the Trinity Monastery of St Sergius, in a heritable estate in Vladimir uezd, in Novoselo hamlet, Kharitonovo village; and those peasants had lived under me also in Vladimir uezd in Okulovskaya, a hamlet held by service, and in Mishurino hamlet. And I, Dorofei, without going to court, have made an agreement with the Trinity monastery scrivener, Ivan Pavlov, about those peasants: I have conceded Trenka Ivanov and Ivashka Bogdanov to the establishment of the life-giving Trinity, with their wives, children and all their peasant property, for eternity. And henceforth those peasants shall be of no concern to me, Dorofei, my wife and children, or my kin and tribe, and we will not petition the Sovereign Tsar and Grand Prince Mikhail Fedorovich of All Russia and the great lord, the Most Holy Filaret, Patriarch of Moscow and All Rus' and the boyars about those peasants because I, Dorofei, have taken 50 rubles in money from the Trinity authorities for those peasants.

But if I, Dorofei or my wife and children, my kin and tribe, shall start to enter [a claim] against those peasants and petition the Sovereign and the Most Holy Patriarch and the boyars, the Trinity authorities are to take from me, Dorofei, 100 rubles in money.

And the witnesses to that are: Larion Karpov, Ipat Vasil'ev Drozhdin and Yuri Semenov.

Yushka Olekseev wrote the note in the year 7128.
And on the back of the note is written:
    To this note Vlas Strelkov put his hand at the request of Dorofei Pisarev and in his stead.
The witness Larko put his hand.
The witness Ipatko put his hand.
The witness Yurka put his hand.

48

This charter of manumission is not to be taken at face value. The document is a compromise between the interests of the two serf-owners, Stepan Ivanov Putilov and Dementii Petrovich Tushin. As return for allowing his peasant girl to leave his estate in order to marry, Tushin is to receive half any offspring of the marriage and, after the death of Putilov's bond slave, the return of his former peasant girl. For his part Putilov also receives half any offspring.

23 January 1624. Charter of manumission by Stepan Ivanov Putilov for his villein Tikhon Il'in Kozhukhov granting freedom to his wife and half his children   PRP, v, 66–7

Now I, Stepan Ivanov Putilov have granted a privilege to my hereditary bond slave, Tikhon Il'in Kozhukhov, and have allowed him, Tikhon, to marry Ogaf'ya daughter of Fedor, a fellow belonging to Dementii Petrovich Tushin. And when God completes the matter and our fellow Tikhon marries that Ogaf'ya, let his wife Ogaf'ya be free for him, Tikhon, according to this charter of manumission. And whatever children God sends him, Tikhon, by that Ogaf'ya, sons and daughters, he, Tikhon, is to have half of those children, sons and daughters, in freedom, and the other half to me, Stepan, on account of their father, to my household.

But if God sends for Tikhon's soul and Tikhon shall die, Tikhon's wife Ogaf'ya is free with half her children, sons and daughters, to all four corners, wherever they wish, and in accordance with this charter of manumission Ogaf'ya, Tikhon's wife, and half her children are of no concern to me, Stepan, my wife and children, my kin and tribe.

And Oleshka Nazarov, a fellow of Ivan Borisovich Sekirin, wrote the charter of manumission the 23rd day of January, 7132. Tax per person 3 altyns.

49

The element of constraint in some agreed settlements is shown here. Such settlements are thus reminiscent of the concessions sometimes made by one owner of peasants to another [see 47]. Even among the serf owners the disparity in power and authority was such that it was evidently more advantageous to agree such onerous conditions as are recorded here, rather than go to court. This document, moreover, shows very clearly the real violence which is not always reflected in our somewhat dry legal sources.

The family as the basic unit of peasant life and as the basic production unit of the lord's estate is shown by Fedot having to replace the peasant Sergushka, if he dies, not just by one of his own peasants, but together 'with wife and children, with all his peasant property and grain standing and threshed'. See also [46].

1626/27. Note of an agreed settlement between the Kurmysh (Alatyr') service tenant Fedot Il'in Lopatin and the Trinity Monastery of St Sergius in the matter of the return of Trinity peasants PRP, v, 62–6

Now I, Fedot Il'in Lopatin. In the last year, 134, the archimandrite Deonisei, the cellarer, the monk Aleksandr, and the treasurer, the monk Pakhnutei, and the brethren of the life-giving Trinity Monastery of St Sergius petitioned the great Lord, the Most Holy Patriarch Filaret Nikitich of Moscow and All Rus', about their runaway peasants, Mitka Malygin and his brother-in-law Ondryushka, and Ivashka Sukhanov, Vaska

Petrushin and Petrushka; and as regards those peasants they had his, the Lord's, holy deed [addressed] to Kurmysh to the military commander about me, Fedot; and in accordance with the Lord's holy deed the military commander from Kurmysh sent a week official about those peasants, and I, Fedot, did not give those peasants to the usher.[1] And in the present year 135 in accordance with the Lord's holy decree that Ivashko Sukhanov has been handed over to the Trinity estate to his old lot; and his holy junior boyar, Dmitrei Bezumov, was sent for Ivashko's wife and property and the remaining runaway peasants of the Trinity, Mitka, Ondryushka, Vaska and Petrushka; and he [i.e. the junior boyar] was ordered by his, the Lord's holy decree, to take sworn witnesses and to take off the wife of that Trinity peasant, Ivashko, and his children and property, and he was ordered to bring to Moscow the remaining Trinity peasants whose names are written in this note and my father Il'ya as guarantor. And Dmitrei Bezumov arrived at my estate for those Trinity peasants and to take back Ivashko's wife, children and property, and with him there arrived for that Ivashko's wife, children and property the Trinity servitor Fedor Kokoshkin with a priest and peasants. And I, Fedot, not knowing they had the Lord's decree, fought with them and shot the Trinity peasant Sergushka Bubenkov with an arrow and shot and killed two horses under Trinity peasants. And on the 12th of February, in the present year 135, the usher Mikita Tolmachov, in accordance with the Lord's holy deed, and the instruction of the Nizhnii Novgorod military commander, Prince Miron Mikhailovich Shekhovskii, and of the clerk Ivan Timofeev, arrived in my estate and took my father Il'ya to Nizhnii Novgorod and took with him five horses of those Trinity peasants which I, Fedot, had taken from them in the scuffle. Against me, Fedot, the Trinity authorities were to take suit for his, Fedor's, and the Trinity priest's and peasants' horses

[1] Note that by this period the terms 'week official' and 'usher' were used interchangeably.

and clothing and every sort of property, to [a value of] one hundred and fifty-three rubles, thirty-two altyns, two dengas, and five unknown Trinity peasants and the Trinity peasants, the wife, children and property of Ivashka Sukhanov and his, Ivashka's, son, Kuzemka.

And I, Fedot, not going to court, successfully petitioned the archimandrite Deonisii, the cellarer, the monk Aleksandr, and the treasurer, the monk Pafnutii, of the life-giving Trinity Monastery of St Sergius that: henceforth they would not petition the Sovereign Tsar and Grand Prince Mikhail Fedorovich of All Rus' and the great Lord, the Most Holy Patriarch Filaret Nikitich of Moscow and All Rus' and their sovereign boyars and clerks against me and my father Il'ya in that matter and henceforth would not take suit or start up that matter; and I, Fedot, am to hand over those runaway Trinity peasants, Mitka Malygin with his wife and children, the grain, standing and threshed, the horses and any sort of livestock and all their peasant property to the Trinity estate servitor whom the authorities send at a date a week after St Peter's day[1] in the present year 135. And when I hand over that Mitka Malygin to the Trinity estate with all his property at that time, they are to give a receipt for that and to question Mitka Malygin with kissing the lord's cross [i.e. on oath]: have such Trinity runaway peasants—his, Mitka's, brother-in-law Ondrushka, Vaska Petrushin and Petrushka—lived under me, Fedot, and are they now under me; did Kuzemka, son of Ivashka Sukhanov, die from my, Fedot's, beatings. And if he, Mitka, shall say on kissing the lord's cross that those peasants, his brother-in-law Ondryushka, Vaska Petrushin, and Petrushka are living under me, Fedot, then I am to hand them over; but if he shall say that they formerly lived under me, though they are not under me now, I, Fedot, am to seek them out and, having sought them out, to hand them over to the Trinity authorities and on handing them over I am to take from them a receipt; and if Kuzemka,

[1] 29 June.

112

Ivan Sukhanov's son, according to what Mitka Nalygin shall say, died from my, Fedot's, beatings, then I, Fedot, am to give[1] for Kuzemka, Ivashka Sukhanov's son, to give the Trinity authorities [one of] my own peasant[s].

And they are to question Mitka Malygin about the wife and children of Ivan Sukhanov; if Mitka shall say [so], I am also to hand her over and the children too. And they are to question Mitka about Ivashka Sukhanov's wife before the image of the Saviour to say on his soul, firmly, before me, Fedot, and before outside people [and what he says is to be] in all compared with what is written in this note.

And the rye grain which they sowed [according to the account] of Mitka Malygin, for the present year 135 I am to allow them to reap, if God grant that it ripen on time; and he, Mitka, is to say whether Ivashko Sukhanov under me sowed rye for the year 135 and, if he says that he sowed, I am to allow him to harvest it when it ripens. And Mitka is to be questioned also to say on his soul: if he says Kuzemka, Ivan Sukhanov's son, died not from my, Fedot's, beatings, but by the will of God, I am not to give my own peasant for him, and if, [as regards] the wife and children of Ivashko Sukhanov, she is not with me and they have no case against me as regards this note for this peasant woman, nothing is to be given for her either, and for all this the Trinity servitor whom the authorities send is to give a receipt.

And I, Fedot, am to hand over to the Trinity servitor at the same time the dark green long dress of Fedor Kokoshkin's servant, the English cloth, the fleece-lined sheepskin coat, the bearskin [coat], cape, rug, two muskets, tablecloth, feather pillow and three horses which remained with me after the usher Mikita Tolmachov; and if those horses have been sold by me or if any horse has been lost, I, Fedot, am to pay for the three horses and for the two horses killed, five rubles per horse, at the date which the authorities shall indicate, St Nikola's day in the autumn[2] in the year 136. As for the five horses of the

---

[1] 'to give' is thus repeated in the original.   [2] 28 September or 14 October.

Trinity peasants which Mikita Tolmachov took with my father, the Trinity authorities are not to ask for those five horses of my father and me since those horses have reached them.

And for maiming and wounding the Trinity peasant Ser- gunka, [I am] to pay 5 rubles of money the week after St Peter's day[1] in the present year 135. And if that Trinity peasant Sergushka dies from that wound, I, Fedot, am to give in place of that Sergushka my own peasant with wife and children, with all his peasant property and grain standing and threshed at the same date as is written in this note.

And for maintenance and bother to the Trinity authorities who had to have for me and for those runaway Trinity peasants two deeds and a week official, I am to pay 10 rubles of money at a date which the authorities shall indicate.

And for the insult to the Trinity servitor Fedor Kokoshkin, I, Fedot, before that Trinity servitor whom the authorities send am to beseech [forgiveness] before outside people and he, Fedor, is to accept my beseeching.

And if I, Fedot, do not hand over that peasant Mitka Malygin with his wife and children, with all his property, the grain standing and threshed, the livestock, the five horses, the fleece coat, cape and rug which are written in this note, the money for the horses and the 5 rubles for maiming the peasant or, if he dies, my own peasant in his stead and everything as in this note; or do not hand over, according to what Mitka Malygin says, his, Mitka's, brother-in-law Ondryushka and Vaska Petrushin and Petrushka; or, if he says that they lived under me, but they are now not [under me], I, having sought them out, do not hand them over; or, if he says that Ivashka's son, Kuzemka, died from my, Fedot's, beatings, I do not hand over my own peasant in place of that Kuzemka; or in accor- dance with this note do not allow them to reap the grain when it ripens; or do not hand over 10 rubles on time for maintenance and bother; or do not beseech the Trinity servitor, Fedor

[1] 29 June.

114

Kokoshkin; then the authorities of the life-giving Trinity Monastery of St Sergius, the archimandrite Deonisii, the cellarer, the monk Aleksandr, the treasurer, the monk Pafnutii, and the brethren are to take from me, Fedot, in accordance with this note 200 rubles of money.

In this I have given this note on myself.

And the witnesses to this are: Zamyatnya Nikitin Fedorov, Tikhon Mikhailov Olferov and Ofonasei Mironov.

And Ivashko Moseev wrote the note in the year 7135.

And on the back of the note is written: To this note Fedot Il'in Lopatin put his hand.

The witness Zamyatenka also put his hand.

The witness Tikhanko put his hand.

The witness Ofonka put his hand.

50

In the second quarter of the seventeenth century there were a number of documents which laid down differing periods for the right of search, the term during which owners had the right to sue for the return of their runaway peasants. This is one of these documents; it granted a period of ten years, although the petitioners, lords mostly with medium-sized holdings, had sought the right to search without any term. The last phrases of the document lay down that cases have to be undertaken against peasants who ran away simultaneously with any other claims; the owner can take suit to obtain: (1) the peasants themselves; (2) legal recognition of their peasant status ('as peasants'); (3) their chattels, and (4) their property (i.e. home, farm buildings, etc., but not land). The second of these items reinforces the impression gained from earlier seventeenth-century documents that the term 'peasant' already virtually meant 'serf'. The distinction between 'peasants' and 'people' had already been made a century before this [see 38]. Peasants and labourers are bound by the inquisition registers, people are villeins held by deeds of bondage.

About 1634–5. Extract from a list of articles containing the Tsar's decree on the term for searching for runaway peasants

PIK, no. 42 (reprinted from *AAE*, III, no. 350)

Extracted from the List of Articles:

In the petition of the gentlemen and junior boyars: when they learn who has any of their runaway peasants, and although those runaway peasants are still within the term of years, they cannot achieve justice concerning these peasants of theirs and the decree; but [as regards] any which are brought to court, much time is involved in bringing the court case to a conclusion, and some of their runaway peasants pass beyond the term of years, and those peasants are withdrawn from them by the term of years [having expired], even without the court; but in previous years, they say, and under previous Sovereigns there was no term of years for those runaway peasants; and would that the Sovereign would grant a privilege ordering the term of years for peasants who had run away from them to be abandoned, and would that the Sovereign might order that those runaway peasants and labourers of theirs be given back to them in accordance with their service and heritable grants and the inquisition registers and extracts, each man to them by what he is bound, and the people[1] also be given back in accordance with the deeds of bondage.

And the Sovereign Tsar and Grand Prince Mikhail Fedorovich of All Russia decreed and the boyars assented; for the Sovereign Tsar and Grand Prince Mikhail Fedorovich of All Russia in his, the Sovereign's crown villages and in black volosts to give [them] back according to justice and the search and the bonds for ten years; also from the Patriarch, metropolitans, archbishops, bishops and the monasteries, and the boyars, chamberlains and people of the council, and the sewers, bearers

[1] I.e. the villeins or bond slaves.

of insignia, the Moscow gentlemen, the clerks and the attendants, and the in-servants and every rank of Moscow people, and the gentlemen of the towns and junior boyars, and the foreigners, and widows and minors, whoever they are, they are to take away the runaway peasants and labourers who ran away [to those landlords] ten years ago or less and to give them back too; but the claimants are to take suit, simultaneously with [their suit against] the peasants, [against them as] peasants and peasant [chattel] property and the peasant's holding; but if anyone starts to sue for peasant property and holdings not simultaneously with [their suit against] the peasants, but separately, they are to be refused and not given justice.

51

This is another example of a deed laying down the term during which runaway peasants could be recovered 'as peasants' [cp. the comment on 50]. In this case it was issued to fill a gap in earlier decrees; the foreigners in the Tsar's service had been omitted from the list of those entitled to recover their peasants. They were granted nine years in which to make claims.

27 January 1639. Petition of foreigners, service tenants of various towns, on granting them justice against their runaway peasants as peasants in respect of the gentlemen and junior boyars PIK, no. 43

I. '...Poles and Germans, foreigners, make petition. The gentlemen and junior boyars of various towns[1] last year in

---

[1] As in the majority of sixteenth to seventeenth century documents the term 'town' implies the uezd administratively subordinate to it.

117

146[1] petitioned you, sire, about the term of years for runaway peasants, in that the runaway peasants were decreed a term of five years; and you, sire, granted them this privilege, decreed the term of years in respect of the Trinity Monastery of St Sergius. But we were not included in their petition, but we serve you, sire, continually in every sort of service relating to the Sovereign'. They beg that their favour be granted 'in respect of the gentlemen and junior boyars to decree the term of years for their runaway peasants and to send a memorandum to the Legal Departments so that foreigners' estates held by service should not go to waste and they should not have to leave the service of the Sovereign'.

Note: 'The Sovereign granted the privilege, ordered justice to be given them in [the case of] runaway peasants and, if they are sought out, to issue [a decree] in respect of the gentlemen and junior boyars who petitioned from the towns.'

The 22nd day of January, 147.

II. The 27th day of January, 7147. In accordance with the... decree of the Sovereign, a memorandum to the boyar, Prince Ivan Andreevich Golitsyn and Prince Ivan Leont'evich Shakhovskii and to the clerks Fedor Stepanov and Timofei Ageev. Poles and Germans...foreigners, service tenants of various towns have petitioned the Sovereign and said that they are in the Sovereign's service with the towns every year continually and, as they say, last year, 146, the gentlemen and junior boyars of the Ukraine and Trans-Moscow towns petitioned the Tsar about their runaway service and heritable estate peasants, that, for their services, they should be granted justice against their runaway peasants for more than the 5 years decreed, as the Sovereign shall decree, and in that petition the gentlemen and junior boyars did not include them, the Poles and Germans, the foreigners. Would that the Sovereign might grant the privilege and order justice to be granted them against their runaway peasants as peasants in respect of the gentlemen and junior

---

[1] 1637/8.

boyars from the towns. And the Sovereign...has granted the Poles and Germans, foreigners, service tenants of various towns, this privilege and has ordered justice to be given them against their runaway peasants as peasants similar to that which was decreed for the gentlemen and junior boyars of the towns. A note on their petition by the clerk of the council, Ivan Gavrenev. And in accordance with the...decree of the Sovereign to the boyar, Prince Ivan Andreevich Golitsyn and Prince Ivan Leont'evich Shakhovskii and the clerks Fedor Stepanov and Timofei Ageev to order justice to be given to the Poles and Germans, foreigners, service tenants of various towns against their peasants as peasants similar to that which was decreed for the gentlemen and junior boyars from the towns for 9 years.

52

This is the first two sections of a lengthy document which formed part of the Instructions Book of the Land Department. The lords with smaller estates appeal for the abandonment of any term to the right of search for peasants and villeins who have run away or been taken away by other lords, but are granted a period of ten years.

The document repeats the difference between peasants and people already noted in [50]. Peasants are bound by the inquisition registers and extracts; people are servile on the basis of deeds of bondage.

23 July 1641. Regulations relating to cases of searching for and removal of peasants PRP, v, 362–5

On the 11th day of March, 7150,[1] the usher, Lazar Beketov, from the High Constable's Office submitted a memorandum

[1] 1642.

to Vasilii Petrovich Naumov and Mikita Naumovich Begletsov and the clerks Ivan Larionov and Aleksei Levlev in the Land Department and in the memorandum he writes:

On the 9th day of March, 7150, in accordance with the decree of the Sovereign Tsar and Grand Prince Mikhail Fedorovich of All Russia a memorandum to Vasilii Petrovich Naumov and Mikita Naumovich Begletsov and to the clerks Ivan Larionov and Aleksei Levlev. Last year, 149,[1] the gentlemen and junior boyars of various towns petitioned the Sovereign Tsar and Grand Prince Mikhail Fedorovich of All Russia against the metropolitans, archbishops, bishops and the Trinity Monastery of St Sergius and other various monasteries against the archimandrites, abbots and boyars and the chamberlains, sewers, and the bearers of insignia and the Moscow gentlemen, clerks and the attendants and every rank of Moscow people and against their brethren, the gentlemen, and against the junior boyars, about people and peasants who run away or are removed and on every sort of offence, that the Sovereign might grant the favour and order his Sovereign's decree to be made for them about people and peasants who run away or are removed and on every sort of offence with the metropolitans, archbishops and bishops and the authorities of the Trinity and other monasteries and with the boyars and chamberlains, and with the people of the Council, and sewers and bearers of insignia, and the Moscow gentlemen and the clerks and attendants and the Moscow people of every rank, and their brethren, the gentlemen and junior boyars. And the Sovereign Tsar and Grand Prince Mikhail Fedorovich of All Russia, after hearing the petition of the gentlemen and junior boyars decreed and the boyars assented; to make in accordance with his Sovereign decree and the boyars' assent [a decree] on murder cases, on people and peasants who run away or are removed and on every sort of offence; and what has been ordered to be made in any of those cases in accordance with the Sovereign's decree and the

[1] 1640/1.

boyars' assent is sent to you in the Land Department under this memorandum.

(1) In the petition of the gentlemen and junior boyars of all towns it is written: their old-established people and peasants run away from them to the Sovereign's crown and to black volosts and villages and to boyar estates held by service and inheritance and to [those of the] Patriarch, the metropolitans, the archbishops, bishops and the Trinity and those of other various monasteries and to boyars, chamberlains and to sewers, and to bearers of insignia and Moscow gentlemen and to service and hereditary tenants of every rank on preferential terms; and those many lords holding by service and inheritance and the monasteries build free settlements on waste places for those run-away people and peasants of theirs, and on account of this their [i.e. the petitioners'] estates held by service and inheritance become empty; and those same runaway people and peasants of theirs, after living out their term of years with those people, and relying on those powerful people, wherever each begins to live, arriving from those people, instigate the remaining people and peasants [to go] from them and set fire to and destroy their homes with every sort of ruin; and on those their runaway peasants and labourers, though one may bind them to one beforehand, they had loan contracts outstanding against them and every sort of bondage deed for large loans and borrowings, and others had acquired by force lands held by service and inheritance and every sort of appurtenance, and people and peasants.

And the Sovereign Tsar and Grand Prince Mikhail Fedoro-vich of All Russia decreed and the boyars assented: to give justice to the gentlemen and junior boyars and people of every rank from whom they have acquired by force lands held by service and inheritance and every sort of appurtenance and people and peasants. But if any people of any rank, wanting to bind to themselves the runaway peasants and labourers of others, had against them deeds of obligation and notes for great loans, and if any peasants and labourers have to be given back to anyone, and those people from whom they take those runaway peasants and labourers start to take suit, according to those notes of loan and deeds of obligation on those people, against those to whom those peasants and labourers will be given back, then those people are to be refused in that, and according to those deeds of obligation for loans, and according to every sort of bondage deed, not to be given justice; do not accept others' peasants and labourers, do not give them loans and do not trust those deeds of obligation and notes of loans; and those notes and deeds of obligation of theirs are to be held in the Department and are to be entered in the registers; and if any peasants and labourers are to be given away according to justice and [the right of] search, they are to be given away with their loan.

(2) In the petition of the gentlemen and junior boyars [it is written]: if they find out with whom any of their runaway peasants are and those runaway peasants are still within the term of years and they are unable to achieve justice and the decree against their peasants, and if there are any before the courts much time is involved in bringing the court case to a conclusion; and some of their runaway peasants pass beyond the term of years, and those peasants withdraw from them in the term of years and from the court, but in previous years, they say, and under previous Sovereigns there was no term of years for those runaway peasants; and would that the Sovereign might grant a privilege, ordering the term of years for peasants who had run away from them to be abandoned, and would that the Sovereign might order that those runaway peasants and labourers of theirs be given back to them in accordance with their service and heritable grants and the inquisition registers and extracts, each man to him by what he is bound, and the people also be given back in accordance with the deeds of bondage. And the Sovereign Tsar and Grand Prince Mikhail Fedorovich of All Russia decreed and the boyars assented: the Sovereign Tsar and Grand Prince Mikhail Fedorovich of All

Russia is to have runaway peasants and labourers in his, the Sovereign's, crown villages and the black volosts, and from his, the Sovereign's, crown villages and from the black volosts is to give [them] back according to justice and the deeds of bondage and the search, for ten years; also from the Patriarch, metropolitans, archbishops, bishops, from the monasteries, and from the boyars, chamberlains and the people of the Council, from the sewers, from the bearers of insignia from the Moscow gentlemen, from the clerks, the attendants, the in-servants and Moscow people of every rank, and from the gentlemen of the towns and junior boyars, and the foreigners and the widows and the minors, whoever they are, they are to have the runaway peasants and labourers and to give [them] back for ten years too, but they are to take suit simultaneously [with their suit against] the peasants, [against them as] peasants and peasant property and the peasant's holding; and if anyone starts to sue for peasant property and a holding not simultaneously with [their suit against] the peasants, but separately, they are to be refused and not given justice.

53

This is an example of a loan obligation where no interest is to be paid unless the capital sum is not returned at the term specified. Such documents reflect the spread in the use of money and come mainly from areas where labour rents were less important. They show that individual enserfment was continuing alongside the social struggle waged by the lords to bind the entire body of peasants and other dependants to their masters.

8 March 1643. *Loan obligation of Danila son of Fedor, a peasant of the Tikhvin monastery, to Gavril treasurer of that monastery, for two rubles*   PRP, v, 58

Now I, Danila son of Fedor, a peasant of the Immaculate Virgin Monastery, Tikhvin, from Chyurikovo hamlet, have taken from the treasurer of the Immaculate Virgin Monastery, Tikhvin, the monk Gavril, two Moscow rubles from the monastery's treasury, straight, without addition [of interest] from the third Sunday in Lent of the present year one hundred and fifty-one. And I am to pay off that money to the treasury of the Immaculate Virgin in the year one hundred and fifty-two on the third Sunday in Lent one ruble, and the remaining ruble I am to pay in one hundred and fifty-three at the same date on the third Sunday in Lent. But if that money remains [owing] after term, then I am to pay interest on that money as is usual among people, six for five, according to the amount.

And Ignatei Patrakiev is witness to that.

And the Transfiguration clerk of the Tikhvin artisan quarter, Filka Fomin, wrote the obligation on the 8th day of March, the year 7151.

[On the reverse:] The witness Ignashka put his hand.

54

In this document the petitioners are granted the right to search for runaway peasants and labourers without a term of years. This right seems to be limited, however, to the Moscow uezd. The order gives us a good illustration of the processes involved in carrying out enumerations of peasant households and of some of the measures taken by landlords to avoid registration or to record 'peasants as people' so as to reduce the amount of taxation they had to forward to the state authorities. Thus, lords evidently transferred 'many households into a single household', presumably on the basis of the definition of a household laid down in 1550 [see 40], because of the changes in the taxation system introduced in the 1620s when the peasant household, not land, became the basic measure for tax assessment. Serfs ('peasants') were registered as villeins ('people') and the distinction between these two categories is made more explicit by the questions to be asked about the latter. Entire households, of both peasants and labourers, were also concealed, buried in the forest, and tenements were claimed to have been abandoned.

1646. Recording order for an enumeration of Moscow uezd

PIK, no. 46 (reprinted from AAE, no.14)

...ordered Ivan Stepanovich Urusov and the junior clerk Semen Nesvitaev to go to Moscow uezd, to the stans and volosts of the Zarech'e half,[1] to the Sovereign's crown villages, hamlets and clearances; and to the heritable estates of the Patriarch, the metropolitans, bishops and monasteries; and to the service and heritable estates of the boyars, chamberlains, people of the Council, sewers, bearers of insignia, Moscow gentlemen, clerks, people of the Departments, attendants, gentlemen and junior boyars of the towns, foreigners and serving people of every rank, retired gentlemen and junior boyars, and widows and minors, for the purpose that: in the past year 153[2] the gentlemen and junior boyars of all the towns petitioned the Sovereign Tsar and Grand Prince Aleksei Mikhailovich of All Russia, [saying that] in the year 153 they were on the Sovereign's service at Tula, and they served his father the Sovereign of blessed memory, the Great Sovereign Tsar and Grand Prince Mikhail Fedorovich of All Russia, in other regiments, thirty-two years, and they also served former sovereigns with continual service; and from their service they have become poor,

---

[1] I.e. the half beyond the river.   [2] 1644/5.

burdened with great debts and their horses have been lost, and their estates held by service and inheritance have become waste and their homes have become impoverished and ravaged, without anything left, from war and powerful people: and, they say, if any of their people and peasants leave them for powerful people, for boyars, chamberlains, people privy [to the Sovereign], authorities and monasteries, the decree of the Sovereign on handing over those runaway peasants of theirs is a term of ten years; but they are on the Sovereign's service every year and are unable to get to know about those runaway peasants of theirs in that term of years; and they allege that other powerful people distribute their runaway peasants for that term of years among their distant estates, and when the term of years has passed for their runaway peasants, they bring those runaway peasants into their estates which are contiguous with them, and they remove their remaining people and peasants from them to their own estates held by inheritance and service and call those runaway peasants of theirs their old-established peasants; and other peasants of theirs, their runaway peasants, they record as living under powerful people in the registers and in notes of loans out of sight, relying on those under whom they live when they run away from them [i.e. the claimants]; and would that the Sovereign might grant them a privilege and order the term of years for handing over their runaway peasants to be abandoned; and that the Sovereign might grant a privilege and order their runaway peasants to be handed over to them in accordance with the inquisition registers and the extracts, as they get to know about those runaway peasants of theirs, and not with a term of years. But in the Law Codes of the Tsar and Grand Prince Ivan Vasil'evich of All Russia, of blessed memory, which were sent from various Departments in the years 47 and 58,[1] it is written: on the 14th day of November, the year 106,[2] the Tsar and Grand Prince Fedor Ivanovich of

[1] 1538/9 and 1550.
[2] 1597. This is evidently an addition made to the copies of these Law Codes.

All Russia, of blessed memory, decreed and the boyars assented:
runaway peasants were to be handed over to the Patriarch,
authorities, monasteries, boyars and people of every rank
according to justice and the [right of] search, with wives,
children and all their property for five years; but beyond five
years runaway peasants about whom there had been no petition
in five years were not to be handed over to anyone; but as to
any about whom there had been a petition prior to the five
years and whose cases as runaway peasants had been brought
to court before that decree of the Sovereign, but had not been
completed, those cases were to be completed in accordance with
justice and the [right of] search. And in the High Constable's
Office there is an extract from the Law Code which was sent
from the Moscow Justice Department and it is written: in the
past year 145[1] the Sovereign's father, of blessed memory, the
Great Sovereign Tsar and Grand Prince Mikhail Fedorovich of
All Russia granted a privilege to the gentlemen and junior
boyars of the Ukraine and Trans-Moscow towns; he ordered
justice to be given them against their runaway peasants as
peasants, according to their petition, against the authorities
of the Trinity Monastery of St Sergius; and at that time the
authorities of the Trinity Monastery of St Sergius handed over
runaway peasants in accordance with justice for nine years. But
in the past year 149[2] the Sovereign's father, of blessed memory,
the Great Sovereign Tsar and Grand Prince Mikhail Fedorovich
of All Russia decreed and the boyars assented: at the petition
of the gentlemen and junior boyars of various towns, who, in
the past year 149, were in Moscow on service, runaway peasants
and labourers are to be held in the Sovereign's crown villages
and are to be handed over from the Sovereign's crown villages
and the black volosts in accordance with justice and the [right
of] search for ten years; and also the Patriarch, authorities,
monasteries, boyars, chamberlains, gentlemen of every rank of
Moscow and of the towns, the junior boyars, foreigners and

[1] 1636/7.   [2] 1640/1.

people of every rank are to have runaway peasants and labourers, and to hand them over for ten years, too; and the claimants are to take suit, with [their suit against] the peasants simultaneously, [against them as] peasants and peasant [chattel] property and the peasant's holding; but if anyone starts to sue for peasant property and holdings not simultaneously with [their suit against] the peasants, they are to be refused the property and holding and not to be given justice; but if any people of any rank, wishing to attach runaway peasants and labourers of others to themselves, have obligations and notes of great loans against them, and if there are any peasants and labourers who are to be handed back to anyone according to the court, and those people from whom they take those runaway peasants and labourers, sue, in accordance with those obligations and notes of loans, those people to whom they hand back those peasants and labourers, then those obligations and notes of loans are not to be believed, but those obligations and notes are to be held in the Department and recorded in the registers, and they [the claimants] are to be refused: do not take the peasants and labourers of others and do not give them loans; but those peasants and labourers are to be handed back with all their loans to whomever is indicated according to justice and the [right of] search. And in the present year 154,[1] on the 19th day of October, the Sovereign Tsar and Grand Prince Aleksei Mikhailovich of All Russia decreed and the boyars assented: let that article on peasants be in accordance with the regulation of former Sovereigns and as it was established under his sovereign father, of blessed memory, under the Great Sovereign Tsar and Grand Prince Mikhail Fedorovich of All Russia, in the year 149, because five years were added compared with the regulation of former Sovereigns and it was doubled, [being made] ten years. But now for genuine information, the Sovereign Tsar and Grand Prince Aleksei Mikhailovich of All Russia has decreed and the boyars have assented: to send

[1] 1645.

into Moscow uezd, and to all towns, chamberlains and gentle-men of quality on oath to the Sovereign to write down the peasants and labourers, their children, brothers and relatives by name, father's name and surname [who live] in the Sovereign's crown volosts and in the Patriarch's, metropolitans' and mona-steries' heritable estates, and with boyars, chamberlains, people of the Council, sewers, bearers of insignia, Moscow gentlemen, clerks, attendants, gentlemen and junior boyars from the towns and with all sorts of serving people, retired gentlemen and junior boyars, widows and minors, and the artisan quarter people, all sorts of artisan trading people in the artisan and trading quarters in towns and whatever people live with the Patriarch and his authorities, the monasteries, boyars, chamber-lains, people of the Council, sewers, bearers of insignia, Mos-cow gentlemen, clerks, people of the Departments, attendants and junior boyars of the towns, and with foreigners and people of every rank as trusted men[1] and any labourers and their womenfolk who live on church lands, and in the uezd, on estates held by service and inheritance. And they are to look to that and guard it fast so that no one should escape that enumeration or conceal peasants and labourers or transfer many households into a single household or record any peasants and labourers of others out of sight as their own or call their peasants people; but if anyone calls peasant households people's ones, there should be enquiries about those people: what people are they and under whom? old-established or bond? and if they say they are bond, then the deeds of bondage of those people are to be looked out; but if they call them old-established, then those people are to be set before you and to be asked about their old-established state, and you are to record them as an item. Also no one in the Patriarch's, the metropolitans', monasteries' or church estates should record their peasants as servants and children;[2] but if anyone should at the recording call their

---

[1] These were dependants of boyars or landlords trusted to live and work in artisan quarters of towns.　　　　[2] Cp. [41], p. 94 n. 2.

peasants servants and children, then they should be questioned about that and you should record them as an item. But it should be said to all people: if any people in their estates held by service or inheritance begin to conceal their peasants or transfer them from two or three households into one household, or out of sight to record the peasants and labourers of others, or in the households to call the peasants their people, then if anyone tells of that and it is sought out directly, then from those people who conceal a peasant or a labourer fifty chets[1] shall be taken from their service tenure or heritable estates to the Sovereign for each peasant and given to those people who seek out who has those concealed peasants: but if any people without cunning misrecord two or three fellows in a hundred, do not hold them at fault for that; but if there are more peasants than that mis-recorded, that is a fault. But where empty tenements are come upon and those holding estates by service or inheritance begin to say that the peasants and labourers have run away from them from those tenements they are to be questioned properly about that and those peasants and labourers are to be recorded, and their children, brothers and relatives with the fathers' [names] and surnames and who ran away in which year in the ten years decreed, but beyond ten years they are not to be recorded. But then they are to be told: if anyone records another's peasant who is a runaway as his own and afterwards that is investigated, they shall be severely punished; and as peasants and labourers and their households are enumerated, then according to those enumeration registers the peasants and labourers, their children, brothers and relatives shall be bound without term of years; and if any are born after that enumeration and begin anew to live in tenements, those households shall not be set up as extra households, because their fathers have been recorded in the enumeration registers; but concealed households are to be sought out and there shall be five years after the enumeration books for that search; but after five years have passed, no peti-

---

[1] For the range of allocations for servitors' estates see p. 21.

tion about concealed households shall be accepted, but they shall be refused this. But if a free man, but not someone's runaway peasant or labourer, comes to anyone in his estate held by inheritance or service and wishes to live under anyone as a peasant, the service and heritable tenants are to bring such free people to Moscow to be questioned and noted in the Service Tenure Department, and for those of Kazan' to Kazan', and Novgorod to Novgorod, the same year that they come; but without registering a free man no one is to accept [him] as a peasant or to keep him under them. But if any people after that enumeration begin to accept runaway peasants and keep them under themselves, and heritable and service tenants seek out their runaway peasants under them, then they are to hand over those runaway peasants, in accordance with justice and the [right of] search and those enumeration registers, with all their property and grain, standing, threshed and in the ground; and they are liable, for those years which they lived as runaways, to the Sovereign's dues and the payments to the heritable and service estate holders and they are to be handed over to the claimant whose peasants they are. But for information the Sovereign decreed that those sewers and gentlemen should give lists over a clerk's note of the names of the villages, hamlets and clearings with the wastes from the inquisitions and revision registers. And to Ivan and the junior clerk Semen a list over the clerk's note of Moscow uezd has been given from the records of the survey and measurement by Fedor Pushkin and the clerk Ondrei Stroev in the years 135 and 136[1] of lands held by service and inheritance. And Ivan and the junior clerk Semen, arriving in Moscow uezd on the other side of the river Moscow in the stans, volosts and the crown villages, hamlets and clearances of the Sovereign Tsar and Grand Prince Aleksei Mikhailovich of All Russia, and in the heritable estates of the Patriarch, the metropolitans and monasteries and in the estates held by inheritance and service by the boyars, chamberlains, people of

---

[1] 1626/7 and 1627/8.

the Council, sewers, bearers of insignia, Moscow gentlemen, clerks, people of the Departments, attendants, gentlemen and junior boyars of the towns, foreigners and serving people of every rank, retired gentlemen and junior boyars, and widows and minors, are to read out this decree of the Sovereign, and not on one day [only], to the gentlemen and junior boyars, stewards, reeves and sworn men, so that the gentlemen and junior boyars and their stewards, reeves and sworn men bring them reports, in their own hands or those of their father confessors, of what households [there are] in those villages, hamlets and clearings and, in them, [what] peasants and labourers, their children, brothers, relatives and neighbours and neighbours' folk by name, father's [name] and surname, and so that they do not transfer peasants from two or three or more households into one household and do not record live houses as empty ones. And after taking from them the reports in their hands, they are themselves to review and enumerate all present of those tenements and the people in them by name; and if according to their enumeration there is anyone surplus to these reports of theirs of those tenements and of people in them, then Ivan and the junior clerk are to tell those gentlemen and junior boyars, stewards, reeves and sworn men in relation to this decree of the Sovereign that they have stolen [peasants], have concealed households and people in the reports, not recorded everything in full, and according to their enumeration they [i.e. the officers of the inquisition] have disclosed a surplus in those households above their reports; and Ivan and the junior clerk Semen are to give them back those reports of theirs and to have from them in their own hand or that of their father confessors other reports in relation to the enumeration registers [which show] the households which are in the enumeration registers present. And at the enumeration Ivan and the junior clerk Semen are to tell all people, and themselves to adhere to that rigidly, that no one should conceal peasants and labourers or steal [them], transfer people from many households into one household, or record out of sight as their own the peasants and labourers of others, or call their own peasants people; but if anyone begins to call peasant households people's ones, those holding estates by service and inheritance are to be questioned, who has what people? old-established or bond? and if they say bond, Ivan and the junior clerk Semen are to look out the deeds of bondage for those people; but if they call any people old-established, those people are to be set before you and questioned about being old-established, how long those people have lived under them and the names of the places and persons from which they came; and those people are to be recorded in the registers by name, as a special item. And in the Patriarch's, the metropolitans', bishops', monasteries' and church estates held by inheritance, peasants and labourers shall, likewise, not be recorded as servants and children; but if anyone at the enumeration starts to call peasants servants and children, they are to be questioned about that, too, and recorded in those registers as a special item. And if there are any villages, hamlets and clearings newly established after the officers of the inquisition, then Ivan and the junior clerk Semen are also to record in their registers those villages, hamlets and clearings and the tenements in them and the peasants and labourers in the households, as a special item. And individually Ivan and the junior clerk Semen are to tell all people: if any people in their estates held by service and inheritance start to conceal their peasants and labourers, or to transfer [them] from two, three or more households into one household, or start to bury [them] in the forests, or start to record out of sight at the enumeration the peasants and labourers of others as their own, or to call the peasants in their tenements their own people, and if anyone reports and that is investigated directly, the Sovereign Tsar and Grand Prince Aleksei Mikhailovich of All Russia orders to be taken from those people who conceal peasants or labourers, from their estates held by service and inheritance, fifty chets for a peasant and to distribute it irrecoverably to those people who seek out who has those concealed peasants. But where they come upon empty houses and those holding estates by service or inheritance start to tell them that their peasants and labourers ran away from those houses, Ivan and the junior clerk Semen are to enquire about that genuinely of those holding estates by service and inheritance and to record those peasants and labourers, their children, brothers and relatives with their father's [names] and surnames, and who has run away in which year for the ten years decreed, according to their reports; but beyond ten years they are not to be recorded. Then Ivan and the junior clerk Semen are to tell them: whoever records another's runaway peasant as his own, and afterwards that is investigated, shall be in disgrace[1] with the Sovereign Tsar and Grand Prince Aleksei Mikhailovich of All Russia and severely punished. And what tenements, in accordance with their enumeration [there are] in the Sovereign's crown volosts and in the estates held by service and inheritance, in villages, hamlets and clearances; and the peasants and labourers in the tenements, and their children, brothers and relatives, neighbours and neighbours' folk, Ivan and the junior clerk Semen are ordered to record all in the registers genuinely as separate items. And Ivan and the junior clerk Semen, for confirmation, are, apart from that, to have through the villages and hamlets three or four men from the old-established peasants, stewards, reeves, sworn men or best peasants, and they are to be ordered to travel with them to those who know the names of peasants and labourers who live under anyone in villages and hamlets; and they should tell the truth about them to Ivan and the junior clerk Semen, so that individually those holding estates by service and inheritance should not conceal peasants and labourers and record people's households as peasant households,[2] and transfer peasants from two or three households into one household, and record live tenements as empty ones; and if in any village or hamlet anyone

[1] To be in disgrace with the Tsar automatically involved various punishments.
[2] Evidently an error. The order of the two items should be reversed.

134

begins to conceal peasants and labourers as his, and not to record everyone as households, they should not cover that up for them, but should tell Ivan and the junior clerk Semen so that individually there should be no concealed peasant and labourer households in villages and hamlets. And Ivan and the junior clerk Semen are to have provision of horses in accordance with the Sovereign's decree, from village to village and from hamlet to hamlet in the uezd where it is required for them according to their commission, from those same villages and hamlets: Ivan to have eight horses provided and the junior clerk Semen two horses provided. In villages, hamlets and clearings they are to record uprightly and truly the peasant and labourer tenements and the peasants and labourers in them, their children, brothers and relatives, neighbours and neighbours' folk, in accordance with their oath to the Sovereign, not negligently, without any swindling, without dawdling, with speed so as to get right away speedily, in accordance with this decree of the Sovereign, not acting for anyone in any matter and from that they are not to have promises and bribes, [to record] living households as empty tenements, to transfer peasants from two or three households to one household and to record out of sight the peasants and labourers of others as anyone else's or peasant households as people's households or peasants as monastery servants and children. But if Ivan and Semen begin to act not in relation to this commission of the Sovereign, to be friendly to a friend and take vengeance on an enemy, begin to record live households as empty tenements, [to transfer] peasants and labourers from two or three households to one household, and the peasants and labourers of others out of sight as someone else's, and peasant households as people's households, and peasants as servants and children, and from that begin to have promises and bribes, or begin to swindle in the Sovereign's affairs, and that untruthfulness and negligence of theirs is investigated, then the Sovereign Tsar and Grand Prince Aleksei Mikhailovich of All Russia decrees that their estates held by inheritance and service shall be taken to himself, the Sovereign, and distributed out irrecoverably; and they, Ivan and Semen, shall be in great disgrace with the Sovereign Tsar and Grand Prince Aleksei Mikhailovich of All Russia and punished without mercy.

And when they have recorded Moscow uezd, Ivan and the junior clerk Semen are to ride to the Sovereign Tsar and Grand Prince Aleksei Mikhailovich of All Russia, to Moscow; and after arriving they are to show the enumeration registers in their hand, to submit [them] to the Department, to the boyar Prince Nikita Ivanovich Odoevskii and the clerk Fedor Elizarov and his fellows.

55

This deed, though about an urban situation, illustrates a form of obligation in which the villeins (in this case the children) receive nothing but their keep.

5 May 1647. Reported deed of gift of his five children in consideration of his debt, by the gardener Nikula Leont'ev to the Novgorod merchants Semen and Ivan Ivanovich Stoyanov

PRP, v, 67–9

On the 5th day of May the Novgorod merchants Semen and Ivan Stoyanov verbally petitioned the military commander, Prince Semen Andreevich Urusov and the clerk Luk'yan Talyzin and submitted with their report and note the note of a gift, so that the note should be ordered to be entered in the registers of the deeds of obligations relating to villeins. And the military commander, Prince Semen Andreevich Urusov, and the clerk, Luk'yan Talyzin, after listening to the verbal petition and note of gift of Semen and Ivan Stoyanov, ordered that note to be recorded in the registers of the deeds of obligations relating to villeins. And the note reads:

Now I, Nikula Leont'ev, gardener, of Novgorod, have given a note to the Novgorod merchants, Semen and Ivan Ivanovich Stoyanov, that I, Nikula, have to give them fifty rubles for my debt [recorded] in an obligation and not [recorded] in an obligation; and I, Nikula, have nothing with which to pay my debt of fifty rubles. And I, Nikula, for that fifty-ruble debt of mine have handed over my children to them, the Novgorod merchants Semen Ivanovich and Ivan Ivanovich Stoyanov, to their house, my son Senka, the other little one in his second year and my three daughters, Natalka, Oksyushka and Ovdot'-itsa. My children are to serve them all in their house till their [i.e. the masters'] death and are to do any work required of them; my children are to be obedient and submissive. Semen Ivanovich and Ivan Ivanovich are at liberty to tame my children by any means if they are at fault and to take them away from any evil. And I, Nikula, am not to interfere as regards my children, or any one of them, nor to petition the Sovereign Tsar and Grand Prince Aleksei Mikhailovich of All Russia about them in any town. And I have nothing with which to give my children to drink and to feed, to dress and to shoe them.

But if I, Nikula, start to petition the Sovereign on behalf of my children and to make a claim as regards them, the Novgorod merchants Semen Ivanovich and Ivan Ivanovich Stoyanov are to take from me, Nikula, one hundred Moscow rubles in accordance with this note. And henceforth such children of mine are bound to them in accordance with this note to serve in their house. And I, Nikula, am guarantor for my children in everything if they carry off goods or run away. And I, Nikula, have given this deed of gift for my children on these conditions.

And the witnesses to this: Grigorei Stepanov, Fedot Nikiforov.

And the public junior clerk Vaska Okhanatkov wrote the note of gift on the 5th day of May, the year 7155.

Instead of Nikula the gardener, at his behest, Grishka Timofeev Deksha, a man of the artisan quarter, put his hand to this note of the gift.

The witness Grishka put his hand.

The witness Fedotko put his hand.

The distinguishing marks of Nikula's children.

Senka has a round face, straight nose, the hair of his head is light brown, the lower part of his cheek is double, he has large round ears, dark hazel eyes and said he was thirteen; his brother Ivashko has a round, white face, the hair of his head is very fair, light grey eyes, arched nose; their sister, the girl Natal'itsa is of medium height, with fair brows; she said she was sixteen; her sister Okse'itsa has a round face, light grey eyes, straight nose, light brown hair and said she was eleven; the other sister of her and Natal'itsa, Ovdot'itsa also has a round face, straight nose, the hair of her head is fair; as to her younger brother, Ivashko, and her sister Ovdot'itsa, Natal'itsa said Ivashka is now in his second year and Ovdot'itsa is now eight.

And on that note, from the merchants Semen and Ivan Stoyanov, in accordance with the Sovereign's decree, [due] on the hundred-ruble guarantee, an altyn per ruble, three rubles in all.

56

In 1649 the Code of Laws of Tsar Aleksei Mikhailovich was decreed. This is a translation of Chapter XI of that Code. In it the term of years for the recovery of runaway peasants was abolished and this meant the binding of peasants to their masters. Even if a peasant was able to run away and establish a new holding somewhere he was still liable, if caught at any time, to be returned to his former lord. Thus, the demands of the landowners for the abolition of any time limit to their right to search out runaway peasants were at last met and the right of search without term [see 54] was now applied throughout the land. In some aspects, it is noticeable that peasants and villeins are now not sharply differentiated; both are dependants bound to their masters, with their possessions, livelihood and even to some extent their domestic lives controlled by the master. Thus the law at last embodied provisions reflecting a reality which, as we have seen from other documents, had already existed for some time.

In somewhat more detail, the provisions of this chapter of the Code were as follows. Peasants and labourers who had been recorded in the registers compiled in 1626 and had run away before the Code was issued were to be returned without term of years (§§1 and 2). Any peasants or labourers who had been recorded in the enumeration of 1645–7, or who ran away in the future, as well as their relatives and property, were to be returned (§9); claims based on this enumeration were valid even though there might be no record in the inquisition registers (of 1626, presumably) (§11). Not only was the peasant or labourer and his family (cp. §28) to be returned, but also any property, including unreaped grain.

If female relatives had married while the peasant or labourer was a runaway, prior to the issue of the Code, their husbands were not liable to be returned with their wives (§3); the male labour force had to be maintained. On the other hand, such husbands, though without their property, had to be returned to their father-in-law's former lord if their wives had run away after the Code had been issued (§§12 and 17); this was a measure intended to discourage lords from inciting peasants to run away and from retaining them illegally. A similar provision applied to widows who had run away and to their husbands (§15), unless the first husband had not been recorded anywhere (§16). Even if a runaway peasant or labourer had married his daughter off to a dependant of a third lord, she and her husband were still liable to be returned to her father's original lord (§18). If a peasant woman married the dependant of another lord, the latter had to make a payment to her former lord (§19).

Torture could be used to establish family relationships of peasants (§22). Any children of the first wife of a widower marrying a runaway were not to be handed over (§§13 and 17). Claims for any property carried off by the runaway were to be settled by the court (§14). If its value could not be precisely established it was to be taken as five rubles (§§25 and 26). Ten rubles were to be paid for each year a peasant or labourer was held illegally (§10). Receipts had to be given for those returned (§4) and such peasants had to be registered in the Service Tenure Department; liability for their taxes was transferred to their rightful lord (§6).

If peasants or labourers ran away prior to the Code, but their lords had not taken suit for their recovery, no such cases could now be initiated (§5). Nor could cases relating to peasants and labourers who had avoided being found within any decreed term of years, or to any agreed deals, be reopened (§8).

If an estate had been sold with serfs and it, in fact, included peasants who had run away from other lords, the seller had to provide substitutes for any runaways returned to their rightful owners (§7); again we see a concern to maintain the labour force, a concern which treats the peasant as if he were a homogeneous commodity or object. The value of this object was four rubles (§25).

The lord had to check the validity of the claims of any arrivals that they were free and had to register them (§20); any lord failing to do so was liable to pay ten rubles for each year he kept a man illegally (§21). Moreover, if a lord kept peasants or labourers who had run away, binding them by debts, and these dependants were then returned to their rightful lord, there was to be no claim for the recovery of such debts (§23).

Peasants and labourers might be hired out, but this could not be done in order to transfer ownership by means of written obligations (§32); the dependant remained under his lord.

Perjury by a lord was to be punished by a public beating as well as by imprisonment (§27). But if a lord admitted perjury and then was willing to return the runaways, he was also liable to return any property involved without recourse to the oath, since he was no longer trustworthy (§29).

As a concession to lords holding by service, new tenements set up after the enumeration of 1646 were not to count for tax purposes (§24, cp. comment on [54]). Peasants and labourers were not to be transferred from estates held by service to those held by inheritance (§30); any peasants so transferred were to be returned with all their property to any new service tenant (§31).

Flight abroad did not make anyone free from his former lord (§33). If dependants of different lords married while abroad, lots were to be cast to decide to which of these lords the married couple should go; the loser received five rubles from the winner (§34).

Chapter XI. The law on the peasants, containing thirty-four items.

1. Any peasants of the Sovereign and labourers of the crown villages and black volosts who have fled from the Sovereign's crown villages and from the black volosts and live on the land of the Patriarch, metropolitans, archbishops, bishops or the monasteries or the boyars, chamberlains and the men of the Council or the chamber and the sewers, bearers of insignia and the Moscow gentlemen and the clerks and the attendants, town gentlemen and the junior boyars and the foreigners and any lords holding an estate by inheritance or service and [those peasants and labourers] are in the inquisition registers which the officers in the Service Tenure Department submitted to other Departments after the Moscow fire of the past year, 134,[1] those fugitive peasants, or their fathers, who are recorded as the Sovereign's, and those fugitive peasants and labourers of the Sovereign, being sought out, are to be brought to the crown villages of the Sovereign and to the black volosts to their old lots according to the registers of inquisition with wives and children and with all their peasant property without term of years.

2. Also should there be any lords holding an estate by inheritance or service who start to petition the Sovereign about their fugitive peasants and labourers and say that their peasants and labourers who have fled from them live in the crown villages of the Sovereign and in black volosts or among the artisans in the artisan quarters of towns or among the musketeers, cossacks or among the gunners, or among any other serving men in the towns beyond Moscow or in the Ukraine or on the land of the Patriarch, metropolitans, archbishops and

---

[1] The fire of 1626 destroyed many documents in the archives of the Departments in Moscow.

bishops or the monasteries or the boyars, chamberlains and the men of the Council and the chamber and the sewers, bearers of insignia, the Moscow gentlemen and the clerks and the attendants, town gentlemen and the junior boyars and the foreigners and any lords holding an estate by inheritance or service, then those peasants and labourers in accordance with law and the [right of] search are to be handed over according to the inquisition registers which the officers handed in to the Service Tenure Department after the Moscow fire of the past year, 134, if those, their fugitive peasants, are entered under them in those registers, or if after these inquisitions these same peasants or their children were entered in accordance with new grants to anyone in registers of allotment or withdrawal. And fugitive peasants and labourers are to be handed over from flight according to the registers to men of every rank without term of years.

3. But if anyone is required to hand over runaway peasants and labourers in accordance with justice and the search, they are to hand over those peasants with their wives and children and with all their property and with their grain, standing and threshed. And the holdings of those peasants for former years prior to the present Law Code are not dealt with; but if any runaway peasants, while runaways, married off their daughters, sisters or nieces to peasants of those holding by inheritance or service under whom they lived, or on the side into some other village or hamlet, that [peasant] is not to be held guilty and the husbands of those girls are not to be handed over to their [i.e. the runaways'] former lords holding by inheritance or service, because there was no Sovereign's prohibition as regards this until the present Sovereign's decree that no one was to accept peasants, but terms of years were decreed for runaway peasants because after the officers [of the inquisition had done their work] in many years the estates held by inheritance and service had changed for many tenants.

4. And if runaway peasants and labourers are handed over to anyone: the Department people of the Sovereign's crown

villages and black volosts and lords holding estates by inheritance or service are to have from those people, for the peasants and labourers and their property, lists in their hand to be held in case of argument. And the lists are ordered to be written at Moscow and in the towns by the public junior clerks, and in villages and hamlets, where there are no public junior clerks, such lists are ordered to be written by the area or church reader of other villages and they are to give such lists in their own hand. But if any people are illiterate, they are ordered that in their place their father confessors should put their hand to those lists, or anyone else they trust of people on the side, but it is not ordered that a priest or reader or any [such unauthorised] person should write such lists, so that in future no one should have an argument with anyone about such lists.

5. But if any lord holding an estate by inheritance or service is recorded in the inquisition registers as having empty peasant and labourer tenements or places in his household and it is written in the inquisition registers about the tenements of those peasants and labourers that those peasants and labourers ran away from them in the past years prior to those inquisition registers, and to date there has been no petition against anyone about those peasants, no justice is to be given as regards those empty tenements and empty places in the household against those peasants and labourers, because they have not petitioned the Sovereign against anyone for many years about those peasants of theirs.

6. But if runaway peasants and labourers are handed over to a claimant from anyone according to justice and the [right of] search and the inquisition registers, or if anyone gives [them] up in accordance with the Code without [recourse to] justice, those peasants, at the petition of those people under whom they lived as runaways, are to be registered in the Service Tenure Department under those people to whom they are handed over; but from those, holding by service or inheritance, from whom they are taken no Sovereign's imposts are to be had according

to the enumeration registers, but every sort of Sovereign's imposts are to be had from those holding by inheritance and service under whom, on being handed over, they begin to live as peasants.

7. But if peasants are taken from any lord holding an estate by inheritance according to justice and the [right of] search and the inquisition registers and handed over from their purchased heritable estates to claimants and they bought those estates from the holders with those peasants after the officers [of the inquisition had done their work] and those peasants were recorded in the purchase deeds [as being] under them, those holding by inheritance, in place of those peasants handed over, are to take from the sellers such similar peasants with all their property and with their grain, standing and threshed, from their other estates.

8. If any lord holding by inheritance or service had in past years a court case about runaway peasants and labourers and the court refused anyone the years [indicated in] the decree [as the term for reclaiming] such runaway peasants prior to this Sovereign's decree, on the basis of the former decree of the Great Sovereign Tsar and Grand Prince Mikhail Fedorovich of All Russia, of blessed memory, and those runaway peasants and labourers were ordered to live under those people under whom they had lived out the years of the decree; or if any lord holding by service or inheritance had made any agreed deal about runaway peasants and labourers in past years, prior to this Sovereign's decree, and in accordance with the agreed deal anyone granted his peasants to anyone and bound them with records or submitted contract petitions, all those cases are to be as those cases were completed prior to this Sovereign's decree and those cases are not to be begun again or renegotiated.

9. But if any peasants and labourers recorded [as living] under anyone in the enumeration registers of the past years, 154 and 155,[1] after those enumerations ran away, or hence-

---

[1] 1645/6 and 1646/7.

forward begin to run away, from those people under whom they were recorded in the registers, those runaway peasants and labourers and their brethren and children and nephews and grandchildren with their wives and children and with all their property, with their grain, standing and threshed, are to be handed over from flight to those people from whom they ran away, according to the enumeration registers, without term of years, and henceforward no one is by any means to accept the peasants of others or to hold them.

10. But if anyone after this Code of the Sovereign begins to accept runaway peasants and labourers and their children, brethren and nephews and to hold them, those holding by inheritance or service shall seek out from them those runaway peasants of theirs; and they are to hand over those runaway peasants and labourers, in accordance with justice and the [right of] search and the enumeration registers, with their wives and children and with all their property, with the grain, standing, threshed, and in the ground, without term of years. And for however many years they live as runaways under anyone after this Code of the Sovereign, ten rubles a year are to be taken for each peasant as the Sovereign's tax and as the income of the service tenants and handed over to the claimant whose peasants and labourers they are.

11. But if anyone shall begin to petition the Sovereign against anyone about runaway peasants and labourers, and those peasants and their fathers are not recorded in the inquisition registers [as being] under the claimant or defendant, but those peasants are recorded under the claimant or the defendant in the enumeration registers of the past years, 154 and 155, those peasants and labourers are to be handed over in accordance with the enumeration registers to him under whom they were recorded in the registers.

12. But if a peasant's unmarried daughter runs away from anyone after this decree of the Sovereign from an estate held by inheritance or service, and after running away marries

anyone's debt-serf or a peasant, or if anyone after this decree of the Sovereign incites a peasant's unmarried daughter [to run away] from anyone, and inciting [her] gives her in marriage to his debt-serf or to a peasant or a labourer, and if he from whom she has run away shall begin to petition the Sovereign about her and in accordance with justice and the search it shall be investigated directly that that girl has run away or been incited, then she is to be handed back with her husband and the children she has borne that man to him from whom she ran away, but the property of her husband is not to be handed back with her.

13. But if that runaway girl marries anyone's fellow or a peasant, a widower, and, prior to her, her husband had children of his first wife, those first children of her husband are not to be handed over to the claimant, but are to belong to him under whom they were born as villeins or peasants.

14. But if the claimant begins to take suit against that runaway girl for what has been carried off, he is to be given justice in that and a decree is to be drawn up by the court as to its decision.

15. But if a peasant woman, a widow, runs away from anyone and her husband is recorded as being under him from whom she runs away in the inquisition registers, individual books or extracts, or in any deeds of bondage, as a peasant or a labourer, and that peasant woman, after running away, marries anyone's debt-serf or peasant, that peasant widow is to be handed back with her husband to that service tenant under whom her first husband is recorded in the inquisition or the enumeration registers or the extracts, or in other deeds of bondage.

16. But if the first husband of that widow is not recorded in the inquisition or the enumeration registers, or in any other deeds of bondage, under him from whom she ran away, that widow is to live under him whose fellow or peasant she marries.

17. But if a peasant or labourer runs away from someone and as a runaway gives his unmarried or widowed daughter in

marriage to anyone's debt-serf or to a peasant or to a labourer
of him to whom he runs, and if afterwards a court decides that
that runaway peasant is to be handed back with his wife and
children to him from whom he ran away, his son-in-law, to
whom he married his daughter as a runaway, is to be handed
back with that runaway peasant or labourer to his former lord
holding by service. But if his son-in-law has children of his
first wife, those first children of his are not to be handed over
to the petitioner.

18. But if such a runaway peasant or labourer as a runaway
gives his daughter in marriage to someone's debt-serf or
hereditary slave, or a peasant or labourer of another lord holding
by service or inheritance, that peasant's daughter who has been
married as a runaway is to be handed over to the claimant with
her husband.

19. But if any lord holding by service or inheritance begins
to let go from his service or heritable estate unmarried or
widowed daughters of peasants to marry anyone's people or
peasants, or anyone's bailiffs or reeves [do so], they are to give
those unmarried or widowed daughters of peasants charters of
manumission in their own hand or that of their father confessors against any future argument. And the payment is to be
had for those daughters of peasants in accordance with the contract. And as to who takes the payment, that is to be written
by name in the charters of manumission.

20. But if any people come to anyone in an estate held by
inheritance or service and say that they are free and those
people want to live under them as peasants or as labourers,
then those people to whom they come are to question them:
who are those free people, and where is their birthplace and
under whom did they live and where have they come from,
and are they not somebody's runaway people, peasants and
labourers, and whether they have charters of manumission. And
if any say they do not have charters of manumission on them,
those holding estates by service and inheritance are to get to

know genuinely about such people, are they really free people; and after genuinely getting to know, to take them the same year to be registered, to Moscow in the Service Tenure Department; and the Kazan' and Kazan' suburb people to Kazan'; and the Novgorod and Novgorod suburb people to Novgorod; and the Pskov and Pskov suburb people to Pskov; and in the Service Tenure Department and in the towns the military commanders are to question such free people about that and to record their speech correctly. And if those people who are brought to be recorded are liable, according to their speeches on being questioned, to be handed over as peasants to those people who bring them to be recorded, those people to whom they are handed over as peasants are ordered to append their signature to the speeches at questioning when they take them.

21. And if any lord holding by inheritance or service brings a new arrival for registration, and has not carried out the proper inquiries, and they enter into his service as peasants, those people are to be handed over to the petitioner according to justice and the [right of] search and the enumeration registers, together with their wives, children and property. And those people who have not instituted the proper inquiries, and have taken someone else's peasant or labourer, are to pay, for as many years as these have been in their possession, ten rubles for the Sovereign's tax and for the income of the lord holding by inheritance or service, for the reason that they have not enquired properly; do not take someone else's [peasant].

22. And if any peasants' children deny their fathers and mothers they are to be tortured.

23. And if any men of whatever rank, wanting to attach to themselves peasants and labourers who have run away from someone else, bind them by obligations or notes of large loans, and these escaped peasants and labourers are given over to someone [else] in accordance with justice and the [right of] search, and they start a petition against those persons on account of these notes of loan and obligations, those who have such

148

loans and obligations and notes are to be refused and not given justice even on account of such obligations based on loans or any deeds of bondage, and those obligations and notes of loans are not to be trusted, but are to be given to the [Service Tenure] Department and recorded in books, and the runaway peasants and labourers are to be returned to their former lords holding by inheritance or service, together with the entire loan. And those from whom the runaway peasants and labourers are taken are to be refused the loan; do not take other people's peasants and labourers, nor give them loans.

24. And if the brothers, children or nephews of peasants of any lord holding by inheritance or service are recorded in the enumeration books as living in tenements together with their fathers and kinsfolk, and, after the enumeration, have departed and begun to live in their own tenements, these tenements are not to be set up secretly, and they are not to be called extra tenements, and they are not to be recorded in the Service Tenure Department, since they are recorded in the enumeration books together with their fathers and kinsfolk. And as from this first day of September in the year 157 no one is to petition the Sovereign about secret tenements, and the Service Tenure Department is not to receive petitions from anyone about this, for in the past years 154 and 155, according to the Sovereign's decree, the butlers and Moscow gentlemen have enumerated on oath the peasants and labourers who are under all lords holding by inheritance and service. And if any have recorded untruthfully, they are sent to those places to take the enumeration again, and for any faulty writing the enumeration takers are liable to severe punishment.

25. And if any people of whatever rank bring an action against someone else about their runaway peasants and their peasant property, and he writes in his claim for the peasants' property 50 rubles or more, or if anyone brings an action against someone for his runaway peasants, and in the petition does not write by name the peasants' property, how much and

what, and the value, and the defendant does not claim the peasants for his own, and the matter is settled in good faith; then, in accordance with the petition, four rubles a head are to be paid for these peasants, and five rubles for blind[1] property; and in the case of larger [amounts of] property it is to be completed by the court.

26. And if any defendant does not deny having the peasants, but as regards property says that the peasant came to him without property, and the claimant says that his peasant came to the defendant with property, and states how much and what kind of property his peasant had, and in his petition he does not write the value of that peasant's property and proceeds to an oath, five rubles are to be put down for such blind peasant property, and the peasants [are to be] taken from the defendant and returned to the claimant.

27. And if anyone in a law-court denies having someone's peasant and takes oath on this, and afterwards that peasant, about whom he has taken oath, turns out to be with him, then the peasant should be taken from him and handed over to the claimant together with all his property, in accordance with the petition suit, and for his fault he who kisses the cross in untruth is to receive heavy punishment, to be beaten with a knout for three days on the market-places, so that many people should know why such punishment has been decreed for him, and when he has been beaten on the market-places for three days with the knout, he is to be put in prison for a year, and not to be believed in anything after that, and is not to be given justice against anyone in any matter.

28. And if the defendants do not deny in court having certain peasants, and it is decided by the court that these peasants be taken from the defendant and given back to the claimant, then these peasants are to be returned to the claimant as peasants together with their wives and any children those runaway peasants have, even though they may not have been recorded

---

[1] I.e. unknown, and hence estimated.

in the inquisition registers, but live together with their father and mother, and not apart from them.

29. And if any defendants in court deny having runaway peasants and their peasant property, and after the oath of kissing the cross they admit possessing these peasants, and are prepared to give them back to the claimant, but, as before, deny having their property, then they are to be ordered to restore the property and hand it over to the claimant, without kissing the cross, since in court they denied everything, both people and property, and afterwards gave back the peasants, but themselves wish from greed to keep their property.

30. And under whatever lords holding by service or inheritance the peasants and labourers are recorded in the inquisition registers, individual books or registers of withdrawal, and are recorded separately in extracts as being on estates held by service or inheritance, then these lords holding by service and inheritance are not to remove their peasants from their service estates to their heritable lands, and are not to let those service estates become wastes.

31. And if any lord holding by service or inheritance shall move his peasants from the estates held by service to his heritable lands, and after that their estates held by service are given to some other service tenants, and these new tenants petition the Sovereign with regard to those peasants who have been moved from the lands held by service to heritable lands, so that these peasants from heritable lands may be given back to them on the lands held by service from which they have been removed; then these peasants are to be handed over to the new service tenants, from the heritable lands back to the lands held by service, together with all their peasant property, and their grain, both standing and threshed.

32. And if anyone's peasants and labourers seek to hire themselves out for work to anyone, those peasants and labourers may hire themselves out for work to anyone of whatever rank, either with or without written records [of the transaction] as

desired. And those people who hire them for work are not to have on them any notes for livelihood or debts or obligations to serve, and are not to bind them to themselves in any way, and when these hired hands have worked their stint, they are to let them go away without any hindrance.

33. And if their people and peasants flee over the border away from any rank of lords holding by service or inheritance from border-towns and, after being beyond the border, then return, but do not want to live under their former lords holding by service or inheritance, and ask for freedom; these runaway people and peasants, after questioning, should be given back to their former lords holding by service or inheritance, from whom they ran away, and are not to be given their freedom.

34. And if their people and peasants flee over the border into the German or Lithuanian lands from any lords holding by inheritance or service who are located in border towns, and beyond the border they marry runaway women or maids of others holding estates by service, and after marrying return from beyond the border to their former lords holding by service or inheritance, and when they come out, and if then their old lords holding by service petition the Sovereign, one about his woman or about his maid, that his peasant girl married that runaway peasant, and the defendant replies that his peasant married that runaway maid or woman beyond the border and in flight, then according to justice and the [right of] search, they are to be given lots for those runaway people and peasants, and he to whom the lot falls is to give five rubles as marriage payment for the maid or the woman or the man because they were both in flight beyond the border.

GLOSSARY

1 ALTYN (*altyn*); a unit of account, six dengas (cp. Turkish *altı* 'six'). See RUBLE.

2 ATTENDANTS (*zhil'tsy*); petty gentlemen attendant on the court and hence of Moscow rank.

3 BAILIFF. See COURT BAILIFF.

4 BLACK (*chernyi*); relating to peasants not on estates of private lords, lay or ecclesiastical, but subject to the sovereign.

5 BONDAGE FOR LIVELIHOOD (*zhilaya/zhiteiskaya kabala*); a contract of bondage with the lord supplying livery and diet.

6 BONDAGE, deed of (*krepost'*); a contract binding a man to his master.

7 BOYAR (*boyarin*); a great noble.

8 BOYARS, junior (*deti boyarskie*); *lit.* 'children of boyars', in fact a lower category of serving gentlemen; petty service tenants. Fletcher called them 'the lowe pensioners'.

9 CHET *or* CHETVERT (*chet'*, *chetvert'*. lit. a 'quarter'):

(1) A dry measure, one-fourth of a *kad'*, which varied in quantity over time: (*a*) in the Kievan period it is estimated to have held 126 lb of rye ($3\frac{1}{2}$ puds); (*b*) for the period prior to the seventeenth century estimates vary between 108 lb (3 puds) and 132 lb ($3\frac{2}{3}$ puds) of rye; (*c*) in the seventeenth century, it is estimated to have held up to 216 lb (6 puds) of rye. All such estimates can only be approximate since this was basically a measure of capacity, not weight; thus, very roughly, it seems to have varied from 2 bushels in the early period to $3\frac{1}{2}$ bushels in the later.

(2) A measure of area; conventionally, the area that could be sown with this amount of seed corn, which was taken to be half a DESYATINA in the sixteenth and seventeenth centuries.

10 CHILD (*detenysh*); a monastery's servant, a peasant who had sometimes grown up on the monastery's land and worked it in return for pay or food.

11 CLERK (*d'yak*).

12 CLERK, junior (*pod'yachii*).

13 COMMANDER, military (*voivoda*); a town or uezd ruler appointed by Moscow.

14 COMMUNE PAYMENT (*protor*); payments made by peasants in communes to an overlord.

15 CONTRACT (*ryad*); an agreement sometimes implying a dependent relationship.

16 CONTRIBUTIONS (*pomet*).

17 COURT BAILIFF (*pravedchik*); an official who executed the court's decision by exacting fines, etc.

18 COURT INVESTIGATOR (*dovod(sh)chik*): a justice, an assistant to volost heads and servants who performed certain legal and police functions, summoned and brought parties to court. Subsequently, identical with USHER.

19 COURT, joint (*sud smesnyi, sud vopchoi*); a court case involving dependants of more than one lord, the income from which was therefore divided between the lords concerned.

20 DEBT-SERF (*kabal'nyi chelovek*); a person enserfed as a result of an obligation (*kabala*). By the end of the sixteenth century debt-serfs were in a similar situation to villeins, but they served only for their master's lifetime and could not be sold or bequeathed.

21 DENGA (*denga*). See RUBLE.

22 DESYATINA (*desyatina*, literally, a 'tenth'); a unit of area, equal to two CHETVERTS; about 1·1 hectares or 2·7 acres, in the case of the official desyatina, but there were also other sizes; on privately held land one such amounted to 1·4 hectares or 3·6 acres.

23 DUE(S) (*obrok*); rent in kind or money.

24 DUE, branding (*pyatno*); a state impost paid when an animal was sold.

25 DUE, cartage (*povoznaya poshlina*); together with the dwelling payment it made the quittance PAYMENT.

26 DUE, customary (*poshlina*).

27 DUE, customs (*myt*).

28 DUE, post-horse (*yam*); maintenance of the post-horse system; perhaps an obligation in kind.

29 ENUMERATION (REGISTERS) (*perepis'(nye knigi)*).

30 ESTATE HELD BY INHERITANCE (*votchina*); such estates in theory could be freely bequeathed.

31 ESTATE HELD BY SERVICE (*pomest'e*); 'lands that are helde at the emperours pleasure' (Fletcher).
32 FELLOW: (1) (*chelovek*); man of low status; servile dependant. (2) (*tovarishch'*) companion, colleague; man of roughly equal status.
33 FIELD: (1) (*niva*); an individual or isolated field. (2) (*pole*); a course in the rotational system.
34 FOLK, neighbour's (*podsosednik*).
35 FREEHOLDERS, small (*zemtsy*); petty non-service tenants (cp. BOYARS, junior).
36 FULFILMENT (*popolnka*); a fairly small addition, often an animal, given with the price specified when a contract was agreed.
37 GENTLEMEN (*dvoryane*); *lit.* men of the court; those distinguished from the great nobles, the boyars, on the one hand, and the peasants and commons, on the other.
38 GOODS (*pozhitki*).
39 GRIVENKA (*grivenka*); a unit of weight, one Russian pound, 0·41 kilogrammes or just over 14 oz; there was also a small grivenka of half this amount.
40 GRIVNA (*grivna*): (1) a grivna (of kunas)(*grivna* (*kun*)) from about the mid-tenth century = 20 nogatas = 50 kunas or rezanas = 480 vekshas (in Smolensk); (2) a silver grivna (*grivna serebra*); equivalent to four grivnas of kunas.
41 HAMLET (*derevnya*).
42 HIGH CONSTABLE'S OFFICE (*rozryad*).
43 HIRED HAND (*naimit*); a peasant or artisan hiring himself out for work.
44 HOUSEHOLD: (1) (*chelyad'*); an ancient term which indicated the servile dependants. (2) (*dvor*, see also TENEMENT); those living together in a house, whether related by blood or not.
45 IMPOST (*rezanka*); possibly a combined transit due and customs tax.
46 INQUISITION REGISTERS (*pistsovye knigi*); the records written by a clerk and resulting from the work of an officer of INQUISITION.
47 INQUISITION, officer of (*pisets*); an official of high rank, usually a boyar, appointed by the sovereign to carry out surveys, etc. with the help of a clerk.
48 INSIGNIA, bearers of (*stryapchie*, see also SCRIVENER); one group of the attendants on the court; they ranked next below the

sewers and included heralds as well as those who on ceremonial occasions carried the insignia of royalty.

49 JUSTICE (*sud'ya*); an official appointed by the Tsar to carry out court cases.

50 KUNA (*kuna*); a marten (fur) or a unit of money. See GRIVNA I.

51 LABOURER (*bobyl'*); an agricultural or sometimes an urban worker, either holding no arable land or, if holding any, often paying labourer's rent, not tax.

52 LIVING (*kormlenie*); local administration was sometimes maintained by granting the official concerned the right to draw income from the population of his area of jurisdiction; this was the system of livings.

53 MANUMISSION, charter of (*otpusk(naya gramota)*).

54 MEASURE (*korobya*, lit. 'basket', 'bin'): (1) a dry measure estimated to be approximately 4 bushels from the late sixteenth century; (2) as a measure of area it was equivalent to a DESYATINA.

55 MEKH (*mekh*); a unit of dry measure, equivalent to the MEASURE.

56 MOSKOVKA (*moskovka*); a Moscow denga. See RUBLE.

57 OBLIGATION TO SERVE (*sluzhilaya kabala*).

58 OBLIGATION, deed of (*kabala*); a contract, often as a result of debt, or the bondage the man was obliged to undergo as a result.

59 OBLIGATION, mortgage (*zakladnaya kabala*).

60 OBLIGATION, verbal (*izustnaya*); an unwritten contract. For an alternative interpretation of this term see [19], p. 59 n. 1.

61 OBLIGATIONS, communal (*rozmet*); taxes, customary dues and other obligations distributed among commune members; also the distribution of such obligations.

62 OFFICIAL (*zakaznik*); anyone entrusted with a commission or given an order.

63 OFFICIAL, court, Boyar *or* Royal (*dvor'skii*); an official of the court (*dvor*) of the Tsar or a great noble.

64 OFFICIAL, week (*nedel'shchik*); an official of the courts of justice, appointed or elected, who worked week and week about with others. His duties, like those of the USHER, were to summon the parties involved, exact fines, etc. In the seventeenth century the two terms became interchangeable.

65 ORPHANS (*siroty*); dependent peasants on monastic and other estates.

66 PAYMENT (*vyvod*); sum paid to lord of a female peasant to allow her to move on marriage to a peasant of another lord.

67 PAYMENT, dwelling (*pozhiloe*); payment due from peasant when he left a landlord; together with the cartage DUE it made the quittance PAYMENT.

68 PAYMENT, quittance (*vykhod*); payment, consisting of dwelling payment and cartage due, owed to the lord when peasant left his service.

69 PEOPLE (*lyudi*); frequently this term was used to mean dependants, sometimes including villeins, servile or near servile dependants; thus it covered both peasants and those engaged in crafts and trades. Usually, though, it meant peasants. In the sixteenth and seventeenth centuries it came to refer to villeins or bond slaves only, since by this time all peasants were regarded as serfs bound to their masters. In addition to these technical uses, the term could be used of people in general, particularly of servitors who, in fact, frequently referred to themselves as slaves of their overlord.

70 PEOPLE, fully bound (*polnye lyudi*); villeins and female slaves.

71 PEOPLE, registered (*pis'mennye lyudi*); those recorded on estates as a result of an INQUISITION or other survey.

72 PEOPLE SUBJECT TO TAX (*tyaglie lyudi*); those liable to state taxation, being neither noble nor servile.

73 POLTINA (*poltina*); half a ruble.

74 PORTION (*udel*).

75 PRIVILEGE, charter of (*zhalovannaya gramota*).

76 PRIVILEGE, terminable (*poletnaya gramota*).

77 PROPERTY (*zhivoty*); especially chattels.

78 PROVISION OF HORSES (*podvod*); this obligation to provide horses may possibly have also included the provision of conveyances.

79 PUD (*pud*); a measure of weight, 40 Russian pounds, 16·38 kg. or 36·11 lb avoirdupois.

80 READER (*d'yachok*); a literate church official, not in holy orders, who read the psalms to the congregation.

81 REEVE (*starosta*); an elected official of a small urban or rural unit. Fletcher calls him an alderman.

82 RENT DUTIES (*obrok*). See also DUE.

83 RENT IN KIND (*uspa*); a term used in the Novgorod area.

84 REPRESENTATIVE, boyar *or* royal (*namestnik*); a deputy appointed to act on his behalf by the Tsar or a great noble.

85 RETAINER (*otrok*); equivalent to squire.

86 REZANA (*rezana*); a coin or monetary unit. See GRIVNA I.

87 RUBLE, current *or* Moscow (*rubl' khodyachii, rubl' moskovskii*); a coin or monetary unit of 200 dengas.

88 RUBLE, Novgorod (*rubl' novgorodskii*); a coin or monetary unit of 216 dengas.

89 SCRIBE (*pisets*). See also INQUISITION, officer of.

90 SCRIVENER (*stryapchii*); a monastic official responsible for drawing up documents, etc. See also INSIGNIA, bearers of.

91 SECTION (*put'*, lit. 'way'); an administrative area or an area of competence.

92 SERVANT: (1) (*sluzhka*); a diminutive form from *sluga* (see SERVITOR). (2) (*ti(v)un*); an ancient term for a man used in the running of estates, etc.

93 SERVITOR (*sluga*). Servitors could be free or unfree. The former were landlords; the latter were often slaves, did not hold land and might act as petty officials on estates. See also SERVANT I.

94 SETTLEMENT, free (*sloboda*); a settlement initially established to attract newcomers by offering them relaxation of obligations, usually by freeing them from payment of the main taxes.

95 SEWERS (*stol'niki*) the highest group of attendants on the court, responsible for serving the Tsar at table.

96 SHARE-CROPPER (*polovnik*, lit. 'halver'); a dependent peasant paying a stated proportion of his harvest as rent.

97 SILVER (*serebro*); rents, loan repayments, etc. in money; (items of) money income.

98 SILVER-MAN (*serebrennik*); one owing rent or loan repayments in money.

99 SITE (*selishche*); a formerly occupied village or other settlement.

100 SLAVE, bond (*krepostnoi chelovek*); a man bound to his master by a deed of bondage (called *krepost'*).

101 SLAVE, female (*raba*); evidently the feminine form of *kholop*.

102 SLAVE, hereditary (*starinnyi chelovek*); an old-established slave not enserfed for a lifetime only.

103 SQUIRREL (*belka*); a squirrel fur or a unit of money (cp. *belshchik*).

104 STACK (*kopna*); a measure of hay, etc.; from the second half of

the sixteenth century the cone-shaped stack of hay amounted
to 4·8 cu. metres or 6·28 cu. yards, being 6·4 metres in circumference and approximately 5 metres up and over.

105 STAN (*stan*); an administrative subdivision of an uezd.

106 STEWARD (*prika(z)shchik*); an intendant responsible, not for as
large an area as a VOLOST HEAD, but for villages or hamlets. In
the late fifteenth century, however, the two offices seem to have
been equivalent, at least as regards the administration of justice.

107 SUBJECT (to tax) (*tyaglyi*); distinguished from 'serving', i.e.
noble or gentle, and from 'non-subject', i.e. servile.

108 SWORN MAN (*tseloval'nik*); a local elected official who took office
on oath because of his particular responsibilities.

109 TAX (*belka*); specific nature unknown, but cp. census TAX.

110 TAX (*kostki*); no details of this particular term for tax are known.

111 TAX FOR THE HORDE, general (*vykhod*); the tax paid to the
Mongols during their domination of Rus'.

112 TAX MAN (*belshchik*).

113 TAX, census (*pischaya belka*); a local payment made to an officer
of inquisition.

114 TAX, marriage (*veno*).

115 TENANT, heritable (*votchinnik*); a lord holding an estate by inheritance. See ESTATE, HELD BY INHERITANCE.

116 TENANT, service (*pomeshchik*); a lord or gentleman holding an
estate by service. See ESTATE HELD BY SERVICE.

117 TENEMENT (*dvor*); a house and its economic appurtenances;
especially a peasant holding. See also HOUSEHOLD.

118 THOUSAND MAN (*tysyatskii*); an elected official responsible for
the armed forces of a town; in Novgorod, a military commander
and justice; his functions were subsequently taken over by the
military COMMANDER.

119 TITHE-COLLECTOR (*desyatinnik*); possibly at first a collector of
tithes, but by the fifteenth century a justice.

120 TOWN, little (*gorodok*).

121 TRIBUTE: (1) (*dan'*); a general imposition on the population;
the basic tax. (2) (*poral'e*) a Novgorod term for the same;
based on ard (*ralo*) units.

122 TRIBUTE COLLECTOR (*danshchik*).

123 TRIBUTE PAYING (*dannyi*).

124 TRUSTED MAN (*dvornik*); a dependant of a boyar, gentleman, monastery, etc. living in their town establishments and engaged in handicrafts or trades.

125 UEZD (*uezd*); an administrative subdivision of the country.

126 USHER, (court) (*pristav*); responsible for summoning the parties involved in court cases, exacting fines, etc. See also OFFICIAL, week.

127 VEKSHA (*veksha*); a small monetary unit. See GRIVNA.

128 VERSTA (*versta*); a linear unit, 1·0668 kilometres or roughly two-thirds of a mile.

129 VILLAGE (*selo*).

130 VILLAGE, manorial (*sel'tso*); a settlement where there was a dwelling of the landlord.

131 VILLEIN (*kholop*); a dependant bound to a lord, often as a result of debt or by a contract, not free to move and not normally able to act as an independent individual in law; 'villeins or bond slaves' (Fletcher). See also fully bound PEOPLE.

132 VILLEIN, fully bound (*polnyi kholop*); a late term which indicated a servile dependant who was bound unconditionally and without term.

133 VOLOST (*volost'*) an administrative area, usually headed by a single authority and sometimes a subdivision of an uezd.

134 VOLOST HEAD (*volostel'*); an official who dealt with civil and criminal cases in the area of a whole volost.

135 VYT' (*vyt'*); a unit of taxation or land measure which had no fixed size until the late sixteenth century, then it came to be taken as 12 chets of good, 14 of average or 16 of poor land in each of three fields.

136 WASTE (*pustosh'*); an area in the forest which had been cultivated; it was then either abandoned, though sometimes continuing to be used for hay or rough grazing, or continued to be cultivated, but without there being any occupied dwelling on the spot.

137 WITHDRAWAL (*otkaz*); the transfer of peasants from one lord to another.

138 ZOBNYA (*zobnya*); a unit of dry measure; $\frac{1}{4}$ MEKH.

INDEX TO RUSSIAN TERMS
IN THE GLOSSARY

volost', 133
votchina, 30
votchinnik, 115
vykhod, 68, 111
vyt', 135
vyvod, 66

yam, 28

zakaznik, 62
zakladnaya kabala, 59
zemtsy, 35
zhalovannaya gramota, 75
zhil'tsy, 2
zhivoty, 77
zobnya, 138

SOURCES

There are few works in English or other West European languages dealing directly with the enserfment of the Russian peasant. J. Blum, *Lord and peasant in Russia from the ninth to the nineteenth century* (Princeton U.P., 1961) provides a certain outline (this work is also available in a paperback edition published by Atheneum, 1965). An older but still readable outline is D. S. Mirsky, *Russia, a social history*. A. Eck, *Le moyen âge russe* (Paris, 1933), gives a useful, though now a somewhat dated survey of medieval Russia and includes translations of a few charters. One important Soviet work, B. D. Grekov, *Krest'yane na Rusi*, is available in German: *Die Bauern in der Rus von den ältesten Zeiten bis zum 17. Jahrhundert* (2 vols., Berlin, 1958–9). The same author's *Kievskaya Rus'* is available in English as: *Kiev Rus* (Moscow, 1959). A survey of Russian agrarian society down to the early sixteenth century will be found in the *Cambridge Economic History of Europe*, 1 (2nd ed., 1966), 507–47; this volume is also useful on west European social conditions. Further information, especially on farming techniques, is given in R. E. F. Smith, *The origins of farming in Russia* (*Études sur l'économie et la sociologie des pays slaves*, II, Paris, The Hague, 1959). M. Szeftel, 'Aspects of feudalism in Russian history', in: Rushton Coulborn (ed.), *Feudalism in history* (Princeton, 1956), pp. 167–82, almost entirely ignores Soviet work.

Among the sources used in determining the meanings of the Russian terms and in suggesting the English translations adopted here have been the commentaries to *Akty sotsial'no-ekonomicheskoi istorii Severo-Vostochnoi Rusi*, tt. I–III (Moscow, 1952–64), and to L. M. Marasinova, *Novye Pskovskie gramoty XIV-XV vekov* (Moscow, 1956). Particularly valuable are the notes by various authors in the series *Pamyatniki russkogo prava*, tt. 1–8 (Moscow, 1952–62); volumes 2–6 of this series are relevant to the documents presented here. M. N. Tikhomirov, P. P. Epifanov, *Sobornoe ulozhenie 1649 goda* (Moscow, 1961), pp. 312–418, contains a helpful guide to many seventeenth-century terms. N. Kapterev, *Svetskie arkhiereiskie chinovniki v Drevnei Rusi* (Moscow, 1874), has proved a useful source explaining the functions of certain officials. E. N. Kusheva, 'K istorii kholopstva v kontse XVI–nachale XVII vekov', *IZ*, xv, 70–96 and V. M. Paneyakh, 'Iz istorii kabal'nogo kholopstva v XVI v.', in *Voprosy ekonomiki i klassovykh otnoshenii v russkom gosudarstve XII–XVII vv.* (Moscow–Leningrad, 1960) are helpful on the complexities of villeinage. There is, unfortunately, no comprehensive dictionary of Russian sixteenth to seventeenth century terms in either English or Russian, but the reports of Englishmen in Russia in the sixteenth and seventeenth centuries, especially Giles Fletcher's *Of the Russe Common Wealth* (Hakluyt Society, First Series, No. 20, 1856, pp. 1–152) and Richard James's manuscript dictionary (published in B. A. Larin, *Russko-angliiskii slovar'-dnevnik 1618–1619 gg.*, Leningrad, 1959) are of some use in suggesting equivalent English terms. A recent facsimile edition of Giles Fletcher's work, with variants, is *Of the Russe Commonwealth, 1591* (Cambridge, Mass., 1966). Another useful account from a similar source is Richard Chancelor, *The booke of the great and mighty Emperor of Russia*, in Richard Hakluyt, *The Principal Navigations Voyages Traffiques and Discoveries of the English Nation*, ii (Glasgow, 1903), 224–70.

Information on coinage is to be found in V. L. Yanin, *Denezhno-vesovye sistemy russkogo srednevekov'ya* (Moscow, 1956), and in F. I. Mikhalevskii, *Ocherki istorii deneg i denezhnogo obrashcheniya*, i, *Den'gi v feodal'nom khosyaistve* (Moscow, 1948). A. G. Man'kov, *Tseny i ikh dvizhenie v russkom gosudarstve XVI veka*, Moscow–Leningrad, 1951, summarises much evidence on sixteenth-century prices; this work has been translated into French: *Le mouvement des prix dans l'État russe du XVIe siècle* (Paris, 1957). The part played by trade in the differing development of serfdom in different European regions is stressed by M. Małowist, Poland, Russia and Western trade in the fifteenth and sixteenth centuries, *Past and Present*, XIII (April 1958), 26–41 and his 'The economic and social development of the Baltic countries from the fifteenth to the seventeenth centuries', *Economic History Review*, 2nd series, XII, 2 (1959), 177–89. See also D. P. Makovskii, *Razvitie tovarnodenezhnykh otnoshenii v sel'skom khozyaistve russkogo gosudarstva v XVI veke* (Smolensk, 1963). Russia's eastern trade is dealt with by M. V. Fekhner, *Torgovlya russkogo gosudarstva so stranami vostoka v XVI veke*, Trudy GIMa, XXI (Moscow, 1952). On weights and measures see N. V. Ustyugov, 'Ocherk drevnerusskoi metrologii', *IZ*, XIX, 294–348, and G. V. Abramovich, 'Neskol'ko izyskanii iz oblasti russkoi metrologii XV–XVI vv.', *PI*, XI, 346–90.

Other items which have been used in the preparation of this volume include:

Antipov, V. Reshenie sporov o mezhakh, *Zhivaya starina*, vyp. I, god XV (1906), otdel I, 129–33.

Betts, R. R. La société dans l'Europe centrale et dans l'Europe orientale. Son développement vers la fin du moyen âge, *Revue d'histoire comparée*, nouvelle série, VII (1948), 2, 167–83.

Blum, J. The beginnings of large-scale private landownership in Russia, *Speculum*, XXVIII (1953), 781–90.

—— The rise of serfdom in Eastern Europe, *American Historical Review*, LXII, 4 (July 1957), 807–36.

—— The *smerd* in Kievan Russia, *American Slavic and East European Review*, XII (1953), 125–9.

Cherepnin, L. V. Iz istorii drevnerusskikh feodal'nykh otnoshenii XIV–XVIvv., *IZ*, IX (1940), 31–80.

—— Iz istorii formirovaniya klassa feodal'no-zavisimogo krest'-yanstva na Rusi, *IZ*, LVI (1956) 235–64.

—— *Obrazovanie russkogo tsentralizovannogo gosudarstva v XIV–XV vekakh*. Moscow, 1960.

Dewey, H. W. The White Lake Charter, *Speculum*, XXXII (1957), 79–83.

Hajnal, J. European marriage patterns in perspective, in D. V. Glass and D. E. C. Eversley (eds.), *Population in history*, pp. 101–34. London, 1965.

Kolchin, B. A. Dendrokhronologiya Novgoroda, *SA* (1962), I, 113–39.

Konovalov, A. A. Geograficheskie nazvaniya v berestyanykh gramotakh, *SA* (1967), I, 84–98.

Leon'ev, A. K. *Obrazovanie prikaznoi sistemy upravleniya v Russkom gosudarstve*. Moscow, 1961.

Nosov, N. E. *Ocherki po istorii mestnogo upravleniya Russkogo gosudarstva pervoi poloviny XVI veka*. Moscow–Leningrad, 1957.

Novosel'skii, A. A. K voprosu o znachenii 'urochnykh let' v pervoi polovine XVII v., in *Akademiku B. D. Grekovu ko dnyu semidesyatiletiya*, pp. 178–83. Moscow, 1952.

—— Pobegi krest'yan i kholopov i ikh sysk v Moskovskom gosudarstve vtoroi poloviny XVII v., *Trudy Instituta RANIONa*, vyp. 1 (Moscow, 1926), 325–54.

Perel'man, I. L. Novgorodskaya derevnya v XV–XVI vv., *IZ*, XXVI (1948), 128–97.

Poppe, D. and Poppe, A. Dziedzice na Rusi, *Kwartalnik historyczny*, LXXIV (1967), 1, 3–19.

Roublev, M. Le tribut aux Mongols d'après les testaments et accords des princes russes, *Cahiers du monde russe et soviétique*, VII, 487–530.

Szeftel, M. *Documents de droit public relatifs à la Russie médievale*. Bruxelles, 1963.

Vernadsky, G. *Medieval Russian Laws*, no. XLI of the Records of Civilization, sources and studies. Columbia U.P., N.Y., 1947.

Zimin, A. A. Kholopy Drevnei Rusi, *Istoriya SSSR* (1965), VI, 39–75.

—— O khronologii dogovornykh gramot Velikogo Novgoroda s knyaz'yami XIII–XV vv., *PI*, V, 300–27.

—— O khronologii dukhovnykh i dogovornykh gramot Velikikh i Udel'nykh knyazei XIV–XV vv., *PI*, VI, 275–324.

—— O smerdakh Drevnei Rusi XI–nachala XII vv., *Istoriko-arkheologicheskii sbornik*, pp. 222–7. Moscow, 1962.

—— *Tysyachnaya kniga 1550 g. i Dvorovaya tetrad' 50-kh godov XVI v.* Moscow–Leningrad, 1950.

After this volume was prepared, *Readings for Introduction to Russian Civilization, Muscovite Society*, selected and translated by Richard Hellie, Syllabus Division, University of Chicago, 1967, was published. This book contains a substantial section on translated documents dealing with the enserfment of the peasantry and the phenomenon of bondage.

GENERAL INDEX

acreage
  a *chet'* (*chetvert'*), 87 n., 89 n. 3, 153
  a *desyatina*, 40 and n. 1, 87 n., 154
  a *vyt'*, 89 n., 160
Afanasi, Archimandrite, grant of immunity to, 60–1
Agrafena of Sheksna, Princess, grants an immunity, 54–5
Alatyr', 110
Aleksei, Metropolitan, 44, 45
Aleksei, Mikhailovich, Tsar, decree on right of search in Moscow, 125–36
  Code of Laws (1649), 138 ff.
Antonov stan, grant of its living, 83–5
  St Nicholas Monastery, 96–8
aristocracy, 1
  black peasants, 84 and n 3
  conflicts among, 26
  control of peasant movement, 18
  delimiting of their competence, 42
  efforts to attract labour, 50, 98
  employment of slaves, 15
  exemption from obligations to, 50, 59, 60–1
  growth of colonization and town building, 14
  increase in private jurisdiction, 7, 8
  labour force of their great estates, 13
  manumission of slaves, 72
  registers of peasants, 15, 42–6, 48
  the *smerds* and, 12
  use of overseers, slave labour, and dependent peasants, 12
  see also under landlords
Assembly of the Land (1649), completes enserfment of the peasant, 25–6

attendants, 25, 117, 120, 150 n. 3
  registration of, 129
autumn tributary gift, 28, 29
Avakumovo, 54

Baltic area, trade with Novgorod area, 26
  and serfdom, 27
Begletsov, Mikita Naumovich, 120
Beketov, Lazar, 119
Beklemishevo, granted to Holy Trinity Monastery, 50–1
Beloozero
  Monastery of St Cyril, 66–7, 68–9, 75
  White Lake Charter, 1 and n. 4, 77
black (*chernye*) hamlets, peasants from, 84 and n. 3, 94, 95, 102, 106–7, 116, 121, 123, 127
Bloodwites, 28
Bolgars, treaty with Rus (1006), 11
Bolotnikov, peasant leader, 23
bond slaves
  change of master, 79–80
  permission to marry, 109
bondage
  deeds of, 78–9, 116, 119, 122, 153 n. 6
  and indebtedness, 121
  Law Code (1550) and, 92, 93
  and peasant registration, 129, 133
Boris Godunov, Tsar, decree on peasant right to move, 101–3, 104
bounds, estate, marking of, 46
  documentary formula, 62 and n. 2
boyars, 24, 49, 153 n. 7
  administration of justice, 81–2
  domination of towns, 33
  labour rent, 93

crown, the
    categories serving, 101–2
    concessions on peasant right to move, 101–3
    decree on runaway peasants, 99–101, 116, 122–3
    foreigners in its service, 117
    land grants by, 21
    as landowner, 8, 48, 94–6
    manorially organized estates and, 7
    Law Code (1649) and runaway peasants, 125 ff., 141 ff.
    new juridical language, 23
    protection of peasants, 94–6
    to be in disgrace with, 134 and n. 1, 135–6

debt-serf, 85, 86 and n., 146, 147, 154
Deonisei, Archimandrite, 110, 112, 115
Dewey, H. W., 'The White Lake Charter', 1 and n. 4, 77
Dmitrii Ivanovich (Donskoi), 56
Dnepr, the, decline as trade route, 13, 16
dry measure, 37 n. 1
    a *chet'* (*chetvert'*), 153
    a *zobnya*, 160
Dubrovskii, Kazarin, 95
due(s) (rent in kind), 43, 44, 61, 154
    exemption from, 59
    grant of living, 22, 83 n., 83–6
due, branding, 85, 154
due, cartage, 92–3, 154
due, customs, 57, 71, 154
due, fodder, 51 and n.
due, post-horse, 44 and n. 1, 49, 51, 57, 60, 71, 154
dues, customary, 40, 45, 51, 57, 59, 61, 65, 71, 95
D'yakon, Mikhail, 86 and n. 2

East Slavs, 1
    custom of early marriage, 10
    disappearance of tribes, 32 n.
    extension of settlement, 10

peasant colonization, 4, 9–10
Easter, food dues for volost governor, etc., 83, 84
Efrem, Abbot, 40
England, merchants' knowledge of Russia, 2
    conditions of serfdom, 7, 8
    execution of Charles, 1, 26
    manorial custom, 5, 7
    wage and labour legislation, 9
    enumeration registers, 130 ff.
    Law Code (1649) and, 139, 144 ff.
Esipov, Vasyuk Noga, mortgage obligation, 58–9
estates
    harassment of peasants, 94
    income from, 30, 65 and n., 66, 89
    use of peasants, 13, 17–18
estates held by inheritance, 118, 121, 125, 126, 129, 130, 131, 133, 134, 154
    Law Code (1649) and, 140, 141, 143 ff.
estates held by service, 20, 87, 121, 126, 129, 130, 131, 133, 134, 155 n. 31
    increase in, 21, 22, 24
    Law Code (1649) and, 140, 141, 143 ff.
Europe, Western
    colonization movement, 4, 8
    contrasted with Russia, 26
    nature of medieval serfdom, 4, 6–7, 8
    origins of serfdom, 5–6
    peasant defence against landowners, 4–5
    and peasant flight, 8
    peasant overpopulation, 4
    population collapse, 26
    under the Franks, 6

family, the
    basic unit of society and economic production, 16, 32 n., 103, 110
    incompatible with slavery, 3

family (*cont.*)
    individual work unit on estates, 16
    normal peasant unit, 103, 110
    peasant flight and, 105–6
    regarded as owner of land, 16, 58
    see also under children
famines, 23, 101
Fedor Ivanovich, Tsar, 104, 126–7
    decree on runaway peasants, 99–101
Fedor Konstantinovich, 66, 67
Fedorovskoe, 69–70
Fedos'in, 77
Fegnost, Metropolitan, 45
feudalism
    development in Russia, 11
    increased power of landlord under, 7
    land transfers, 6
    field, 87 n. 1, 89 n. 4, 155
Filaret, Patriarch of Moscow, 107,
    108, 110, 112
Filip, Metropolitan of All Rus', 74–5
fines, 102
    for concealing peasants, 133–4
    for harbouring runaways, 106
    a source of income, 28
fish, white, 89 and n. 2
fishing rights, 54–5
    income from, 89 and n. 2
Fletcher, Giles (?1549–1611)
    his 'lowe pensioners', 68 n.
    Of the Russe Common Wealth, 2 n.,
    10
    use of term 'villein', 10, 19
foreigners
    and recovery of runaway peasants,
    117–19, 127
    registration of, 129
forests (tenements)
    concealment of households, 125,
    133
    dwelling payments, 81, 82, 91, 92
    increased rate of settlement, 46, 47,
    50, 53
France
    chartes-lois, 5
    retrait lignager, 58

free men
    manumission charters and, 147–8
    registration of, 131

gentlemen, 24, 25, 102, 131, 155
    Law Code (1649) and, 141 ff.
    registration of, 129
    and runaway peasants, 99–100,
    116–19, 120–3, 125–36 *passim*
Germany, Western, 5, 117
Gilevo waste, 52
Golden Horde, 43 and n. 1, 48
    tax liability to, 64, 65
Golitsyn, Prince Ivan Andreevich,
    118, 119
Goluzino waste, 54
Gorodets, 34
Gorodskoi stan, 56
Gotland, 29 n. 1
Great Eve, 78 and n. 2
Grigori, Archimandrite, 61

Hakluyt, Richard (?1552–1616), *Prin-
    cipal Navigations Voyages...*,
    2 n. 1
Hermogen, Patriarch, 103
horseless peasants, 40
    distinguished from 'big people', 39
households (*dvor*)
    basic measure for tax assessment,
    125
    concealment of, 130–1, 132
    definition of, 29, 91–2, 125, 155
    Law Code (1649) and, 143
    process of enumeration, 124, 130
    reduction in to avoid taxation, 91,
    125, 129–36 *passim*
    reports of, 132
Hundred Man, 51, 60, 71, 77, 102, 106

Ignatii, Abbot of St Cyril, 75–6
illiteracy, 143
income, from estates, 30, 65 and n.,
    66, 89
    calculation of, 89 n. 1
income, petty, 89 and n. 1

living, grants of, 83–5
  meaning of, 83 n. 1, 156
loan, payment of interest
  by harvest, 66
  in hay, 58
  obligation to serve and, 86
  by working off, 66, 85
  see also indebtedness
Lopatin, Fedot Il'in, agreed settlement on runaway peasants, 110–
  15
Luka, 95
  waste, 58–9
Lukhovets, 43

manumission, right of, 80
  charters of, 81, 109–10, 147, 156 n.
  53
  fees for, 81
  on marriage, 109–10, 147
  of widows, 105–6
marriage
  after flight abroad, 140, 152
  control of by lords, 24
  customs in E. Europe, 10, 26, 103
  disposition of offspring, 109–10
  Law Code (1649) and, 139, 142,
  145–6, 146–7
  peasant flight and, 105
  taxation for, 28
Medna village, purchase of, 47
Men'shii, Prince Ignatii, charters of
  privilege, 75–6
'Michael the deacon', 86 n. 2
Mikhail Fedorovich, Tsar, 108, 112,
  116, 120, 125, 128, 144
  decree on runaway peasants, 127,
  128, 144, 145
measure, 37 n. 1, 156 nn. 54, 55
Mikhail Andreevich, Prince
  deeds forbidding withdrawal of
  peasants, 66–7, 68–9
Mikhail Yaroslavich, Prince, treaty
  with Novgorod, 34–6
mileage, a versta, 92 and n., 160
military service, 45

crown land grants and, 21
  efforts to avoid, 63
  and landlord absenteeism, 22–3, 98,
  125–6
  and serfdom, 27
monasteries
  attraction of peasants, 68
  gifts to, 29–32, 46
  as money-lenders, 21, 31, 93–4,
  96–8, 124
  and peasant flight, 99–101, 107,
  120–1, 123, 125
  peasant obligations to, 12, 18, 39–41
  recording of peasants as servants
  and children, 94 n. 2, 129 and n. 2
  refectory custom, 29 and n. 3
  registration of peasants, 129
  removal of peasants from, 66, 69–
  70, 75–6
  testamentary benefactions, 74
  tributes to, 28–9
monasteries
  Boris and Gleb, 44
  Emperor Constantine, Vladimir,
  Charter given by Metropolitan
  Kiprian, 40–1
  Holy Trinity of St Sergius: control
  of peasant labour, 18, 19, 69–70;
  grant of immunity, 54–5; mortgage obligation to, 58–9; privilege granted to, 50–1; right to
  withdraw peasants, 62, 63; and
  runaway peasants, 110–15, 118,
  120, 121, 127; transference of
  peasants to, 107–8
  Immaculate Virgin, Simonov,
  grants of immunity, 60–1, 124
  St Cyril of Beloozero, 66–7, 68–9,
  75–8
  St George, Novgorod; peasant
  agreement with, 61–2; receives
  Buitse village as tribute, 28–9;
  testamentary gift from Kliment,
  31–2
  St Nicholas, 96–8
  St Nikola, 54–5, 75

174

Odoevskii, Prince Nikita Ivanovich, 136
official, week, interchangeable with 'usher', 111 n., 114, 156
official, withdrawal, 95, 100
Oleksei, Metropolitan, 43, 44
Onanya, Nastasiya, deed of bondage, 78–9
Onega river, portage dues, 66
Oparin, Klim, 38, 39

payments, 13, 147, 157
payments, dwelling, 81, 82, 157
  for bachelors, 103, 105
  Law Code (1550) and, 91–3, 95
  and peasant flight, 102, 104, 105
peasant risings, 11, 12, 23, 33
peasantry:
  general: ability to write, 16, 52; attempts to define their obligations, 37, 80; concessions during 1606 famine, 101–3; concessions during Time of Troubles, 23–4; development of feudally dependent class, 10; and disposition of the land, 16, 21–2, 38–9; early enserfment, 5–6; evidence of unlimited movement, 47–8; final phases of complete enserfment, 25–7, 123, 138 ff.; high status of free class, 12, 16, 26; increase in impositions and restrictions, 27; increased control by central authority, 20, 22; mobility encouraged by land abundance, 8; organization into village communities, 4–5; ownership of heritable lands, 16 and n., 52; relationship with landlords, 4, 15, 17, 27, 80; remission of right of departure, 23, 98, 101; restrictions on their movement, 4, 16, 18–20, 23, 27, 47, 66, 69, 70, 75–8, 80; selling themselves into bondage, 92, 93; social situation under Franks, 6; sold or con-

ceded from one estate to another, 24, 105, 107–8; terminology of social categories, 24; use of phrase 'beginning to live', 16–17, 58–9, 65 and n., 121; value of, 140
arrivals (newcomers), 18, 87, 88; exemption from obligations, 50, 51, 56, 57, 59, 60; Law Code (1649) and, 140, 148; peasant flight and, 106; tribute-paying, 70, 71
contract, 19, 68
fully-enslaved, 17; disposition in wills, 72, 73–4
orphans, 15, 19, 24, 25, 32; exemption from taxes, 57; use of term on estates, 38, 39, 40, 41, 57 n. 1
'people', use of term, 15, 19, 24, 25, 32, 69, 115, 116 and n., 157; conditions of withdrawal from monasteries, 77; differentiated from peasants, 87, 88, 115, 119, 121; efforts to conceal, 130; freedom from obligations, 59; old-established and bond, 129, 130; on estates 39; recording of peasants as, 124, 125, 129, 133, 134; registration of, 42, 44; restrictions on movement, 75–6; right of monasteries to reclaim, 63; runaway, 72, 74, 98; used to mean servitors, 98
runaway, 4, 8, 72, 74, 98; foreigners right of recovery, 117–19; from excessive impositions, 17, 53, 98; from havoc caused by *oprichnina*, 22, 96, 98; Land Department and, 119–23; Law Code (1649) and, 138 ff.; registration and enumeration, 129 ff.; right to search for, 23, 25, 98–101, 103–15; 115–23, 124 ff.
servile dependants (*kholopy*), 19, 29, 72

177

St Nikola's Day, 113
St Peter's Day, summer quarter day,
  33 and n. 1, 35, 40 and n. 2, 112,
  114
  food dues for volost governor, etc.,
    83-4
  payment to Church, 45
  right of removal, 68-9
section, 67 and n. 1, 158
Semenikovo waste, 52
serfdom
  distinguished from slavery, 3
  final accomplishment, 25-7
  increase under feudalism, 6-7
  origins in slavery, 5-6
  social factors causing, 3
  in Western Europe, 4, 5-6
serfs
  equated with peasants, 25, 115
  evolution of term ('servus'), 11-12
  legitimized designation, 3
  registered as people, 125
servant, 158
  food dues at Christmas and Easter,
    84
servant, monastery (sluga), 94 n. 2,
  99, 100, 129, 158
servitors, 158 n. 92
  conflict with boyars over labour,
    22-3
  increased pressure by, 22
  land allotments to, 21-2 (Table
    p. 21), 130 and n.
  right to move peasants, 23-4
  social categories, 24
  struggle for labour, 98
settlement of disputes,
  element of constraint in agree-
    ments, 110 ff.
settlements, free (slobody), 18, 35
  n.1, 53, 54, 68-9, 121, 158
settlements, size of, 15
sewers
  registration of, 129
  and runaway peasants, 116, 120-3
  passim, 125-36 passim, 158

Shakhovskii, Prince Ivan Leont'evich,
  118, 119
share-croppers, 4, 158
  legal rights, 33, 36
  payment of harvest as interest, 66,
    67
  peasant category, 66
  restriction of movement, 18-19,
    67, 68-9
Shatur, 65
Shekhovskii, Prince Miron Mikhailovich, 111
Sheksna, the, 54
Siberia, 25
silver, meaning of, 65-6, 78 and n. 1,
  158
silver-man see under peasantry
Simonov, Monastery of the Immaculate Virgin, 60-1
slavery
  category of 'villeins', 10
  conversion into serfdom, 5-6
  deed of, 78-9
  distinguished from serfdom, 3
slaves
  change of master, 79-80
  flight by, 80
  full bondage, 78-9
  hereditary, 147
  legal rights, 36
  manumission, 72
Smolensk, 29 n. 1, 35 n. 3, 87
  category of dedichi peasants,
    16 n.
sokha
  implement of cultivation, 33 and
    n. 2
  unit of land, taxation, 83 and n. 2,
    89
Sosnyaga, 54
Spain, serfdom in, 7
stan, 50 and n., 159
  people, 57 and n. 2
state, the
  co-operation with landlords, 8,
    9

178

state, the (*cont.*)
    effect of its development on
        peasantry, 17
    and enserfment, 5, 8
    its increasing control, 20, 22, 83
    payment of taxes to, 3
Stefanida, widow, granted an im-
    munity, 71–2
steward, 51, 72, 102, 159
    complaint against, 38
    and peasant concealment, 134
    and peasant flight, 99–101, 107
Stoyanov, Semen and Ivan, gift of
    children to, 136–8
Sunbul, Fedor Ivanovich, 86
Suzdal', 35
    becomes the centre, 13
    Mongol invasions and, 14
sworn men, 134, 159
Syrkov, Fedor, 95–6

Tatars, 48
    defeat of, 80
    defence against, 63
    escape of villeins, 80, 82
    tribute to, 42, 45
tax (*kostki*), 57
tax, census, 51, 57, 159
tax, court, 57
tax, goods, 71
tax, marriage, 28, 159
tax, mowing, 51 and n.
tax for the Horde, 14 n., 64, 65, 159
tax man (*belshchik*), 43 and n. 2
tax unit
    sokha, 33 and n. 2, 83 and n. 2
    vyt', 89 n. 2, 160
taxation, 3, 102
    assessment after inquisition, 48
    avoidance by landlords, 124–5
    change in basic unit, 125
    immunity grants and, 57
    Law Code (1649) and, 140
    peasant liability, 12, 19, 71 n., 72, 81
    peasant registration and, 70, 148
    reduction of households and, 91, 125

relaxation to attract labour, 18
and social categories, 24, 71 n.
tenant, hereditary, 121, 159
tenant, service, 99–101, 103, 159
    concession of, 107–8
    Law Code (1649) and, 145, 146–7,
        151
    right to recover runaways, 117–19,
        121
tenements, 60, 92, 159
    dwelling payments, 81, 82, 91, 103
    efforts to conceal peasants, 125, 130,
        135
    increase in holdings, 16, 26
    Law Code (1649) and, 143, 149
    without arable, 87, 88, 89
terminable privileges, 20
    and indebtedness, 66, 67 n. 2, 70,
        85, 86, 90
    and runaway peasants, 116, 122
terminal dates, 68
Tikhvin, Immaculate Virgin Mona-
    stery, 124
tithe-collector, 44 and n. 4, 45, 159
Toropets register, 87–8
Torzhok, 36
towns
    artisan quarters, 129 and n., 138
    domination by boyars and merch-
        ants, 33
    halt in their development, 15, 26
    registration of peasants, 129
    treaties with princes, 33
    use of word in documents, 117 and
        n., 118, 119, 120, 121
tribes, superseded by princedoms, 16
tribute paying, 159
    exemption from, 50, 59, 70, 71
    imposition after inquisition, 49
    payment of, 57, 65
trusted men, 129 and n., 160
Tsarko, Abbot, 40, 41
Tula (crown estate), 125
'turfed into full bondage', 78 and
    n. 3
Turkey, 27

179